DAVE LANDRY
ON SWING TRADING

DAVE LANDRY
ON SWING TRADING

David Landry

M. GORDON PUBLISHING GROUP
Los Angeles, California

ISBN 1-893756-09-2

Printed in the United States of America

Cover design by Conrad Kalil. Cover photo by Daniel Lincoln/Liaison. The book was typeset in Palatino by Judy Brown.

*To Marcy, for believing in me
even when I didn't believe in myself.*

CONTENTS

∎ ∎

APPENDIX   **211**

PREFACE

I have a confession. I am a trading-method "junkie." I buy, or at least used to buy, every book on trading published. When a book would arrive, I'd take the phone off the hook, pull down the shades and was **not** to be disturbed. I'd tear into it like an addict long overdue for a fix. When I'd read the introduction about how great the book was going to be, I'd feel my pulse quicken as I thought of how much money I'd make applying the concepts.

Then, slowly but surely, I'd feel myself let down as none of the promise materialized. Authors had methods that were extremely complex and difficult to understand. Further, they were purposely vague. And worse, many, at the end of the book, would assure me that if I spent another thousand or so on a trading course, then I'd really get the concepts.

When Larry Connors, CEO of TradingMarkets.com and M. Gordon Publishing, approached me to do a book, I told him "Great! I've got these theories." After a moment of uncomfortable silence, Larry suggested, "Why don't you write about exactly what you do in a clear, concise manner? After all, this is what you do on the Website and what people have come to expect from you."

At this point, it hit me. I was on the verge of writing a book long on theory and short on substance. A book not unlike the trading books I loathed.

I began to think, what type of book would I want to buy? With that thought in my head, I began writing about my *exact* techniques I use day in and day out in my trading and market analysis. These techniques are not rocket science. If you're looking for a book with complex magic formulas, then you'll surely be disappointed. However, if you're interested in a simple, straightforward approach to swing trading, then this book is for you.

ACKNOWLEDGMENTS

• •

In markets, many often come to the same conclusion through observation and experience. Over the years, I've come up with many "discoveries," only to later find out that others have come to the same conclusion years prior. I have strived to give credit where credit is due to those that have influenced me. For those of you who have come to similar conclusions and are not recognized, I can assure you, it's simply an oversight and I apologize.

The following people have had a material impact not only on this book but also on me, as well as my life. Words alone cannot thank them enough.

Me being where I am was set off by a chain of events six years ago. A chain of events started by Joe Calandro who convinced me that my research was worthy.

To Larry Connors, for teaching me how to think "conceptually correct" when it comes to the markets. Also, for pushing me to excel and forcing me to recognize untapped talent, and for providing me with numerous opportunities.

To Jeff Cooper, for teaching me how to read charts and for showing me you can make a living trading stocks on a short-term basis. To those of you familiar with Jeff's works, you'll notice his influence throughout this manual.

To my futures broker, Rob Lingle, for giving me the same respect given to large traders back when I was just getting started.

To Ken Brown for teaching me to approach trading as a business and for making me a principal in his firm.

To my parents Anna Marie and Sentive Joseph (S.J.) Landry, for putting up with me and all my endeavors over the years.

To my step-daughter Suzie for making me "daddy." And to my daughter Isabelle for always greeting me with a big smile and open arms even on days when I violate my risk-loss parameters. Both of you bring so much joy to my life.

The following people were instrumental in creating this book. Without them, it would never have happened. First and foremost, to the staff of M. Gordon Publishing especially Danilo Torres and Andy Splichal for their work in getting this book published. Thanks also to my editor Judy Brown of Brown Enterprises and proofreaders Jim Johnson, Duke Heberlein, Jason Meyer and Marianne Winfield.

To John Del Gaudio for giving me the perspective of an aspiring, novice trader and for not letting me gloss over anything.

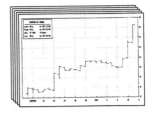

INTRODUCTION

■ ■

Natural ebbs and flows of markets occur over time. Markets often thrust, rest and thrust again. Many times these thrusts can be substantial but, unfortunately, are short lived. In fact, based on research conducted by hedge fund manager Mark Boucher, 70% of a market's moves occur in 20% of the time. The rest of the time, markets consolidate by trading back-and-forth to "digest" their gains. The intermediate-term trader is willing to sit through these periods for weeks to months. On the other hand, the nimble swing trader carefully picks his spots and is able to capture the crux of a market's move without the excessive risks of longer-term market exposure.

At the other end of the spectrum from the intermediate-term trader is the daytrader. Daytraders avoid carrying positions overnight for fear of large adverse market moves. However, as professional trader Jeff Cooper states, "surprises often happen in the direction of the trend." I'll take this one step further and say that surprises happen in the direction of the trend *over several days*. And, by holding positions for two to seven days, substantial market moves can often be captured. The exact reason that daytraders do not take positions home—for fear of overnight surprises—is the exact reason that I do swing trade. Referring to Figure I.1 of Intel (INTC), notice that the stock had rolled over and had began to downtrend. Also notice that it set up and triggered an entry as a Bow Tie (explained in detail in Chapter 7) the same day they announced (after the close) that they would have an earnings shortfall. The stock implodes overnight and trades lower over the next seven days.

FIGURE I.1

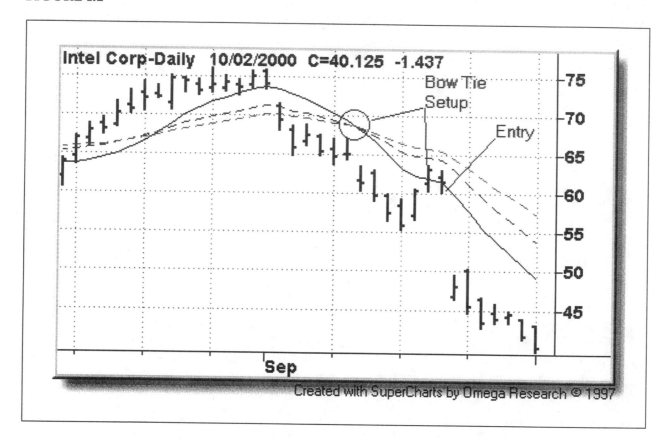

This is not to say that all positions will lead to huge "surprises" overnight. Like all styles of trading, the results of swing trading are skewed. That is, the majority of the profits come from the minority of the trades. You win some, you lose some and through a consistent approach and exercising strict money management, you position yourself to capture extraordinary market moves.

This manual is intended to be a complete treatise on momentum-based swing trading. It is based on my passion for the markets and over 10 years of research and trading. Although I have strived to keep the methods as simple as possible, if you are new to trading, you might want to study the glossary found in the Appendix before getting started. Looking ahead, in Section One, I cover the basics of swing trading including drawdown, rules and money management, straightforward methods for identifying trends and pullbacks. After years of searching for the "Holy Grail" of trading, I have returned to these time-proven basics. In fact, 90% of my trading and market analysis is based upon the concepts covered here. In Section Two, I discuss more specific setups for swing trading. These include Fakeouts and False Moves which allow the swing trader to take advantage of traders who have been knocked out or are trapped on the wrong side of the market; Bow Ties, which seek to capture a transition in the trend without the pitfalls associated with top and bottom picking; and Micro Patterns, which are smaller, yet quite often effective, versions of classical technical analysis patterns. In Section Three, Volatility, I'll show how volatility can be combined with basic and advanced concepts discussed in the manual to capture large moves in stocks. In Section Four, Market Timing, I show how to combine the patterns, setups and concepts discussed in the manual with the overall market. I'll also show three swing-trading systems developed for the index futures. By implementing these techniques, you will stack the odds in your favor by trading on the correct side of the market. In Section Five, Options, I will show how the swing trader can used options to help control risks and maximize profits. In Section Six, Psychology, I will discuss how to recognize and avoid the psychological pitfalls associated with trading. I will also discuss lessons learned through my own experience and those of others. Finally, in Section Seven, I will tie everything together by discussing nightly preparation, as well as providing numerous examples and some additional thoughts on swing trading. In the Appendix, I provide all the formulas mentioned throughout the manual along with a primer on shorting stocks for those new to trading.

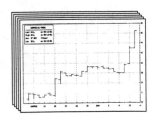

SECTION ONE

THE BASICS OF
SWING TRADING

= =

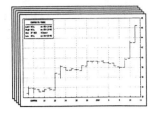

CHAPTER 1

DRAWDOWN: THE TRADER'S WORST ENEMY

You cannot get ahead while you are getting even.

— Dick Armey

All the setups and concepts in this manual, or any trading manual for that matter, are completely worthless without following general rules and proper money management. This can best be demonstrated through the study of drawdown.

Drawdown is simply the amount of money you lose trading, expressed as a percentage of your total trading equity. If all your trades were profitable, you would never experience a drawdown. Drawdown does not measure overall performance, only the money lost while achieving that performance. Its calculation begins only with a losing trade and continues as long as the account hits new equity lows.

Maximum Drawdown or Peak-to-Trough Drawdown is the largest percentage drop in your account between equity peaks. In other words, it's how much money you lose until you get back to breakeven. If you began with $10,000 and lost $4,000 before getting back to breakeven, your maximum drawdown would be 40%. Keep in mind that no matter how much you are up in your account at any given time—100%, 200%, 300%—a 100% drawdown will wipe out your trading account.

Recovering from a drawdown can be extremely difficult and illustrates why money management is so important. Those new to trading believe that if they lose 10%, they will be back to breakeven on the first 10% gain. Unfortunately, this is not true. In order to make back a 10% loss, you must make at least 11.11% on your remaining equity. Even worse is that as the drawdowns deepen, the recovery percentage begins to grow geometrically. For example, a 50% loss requires a 100% return just to get back to break even. This is illustrated in Table 1.1 and Figure 1.1 below. I strongly urge you to make a copy of these figures and paste them near your trading desk.

Professional traders and money mangers are well aware of how difficult it is to recover from drawdowns. Those who succeed long term have the utmost respect for risk. They get on top and stay on top, not by being gunslingers and taking huge risks, but by controlling risk through proper money management. Sure, we all like to read about famous traders who parlay small sums into fortunes, but what these stories fail to mention is that many such traders, through lack of respect for risk, are eventually wiped out.

TABLE 1.1

% Loss of Capital	% of Gain Required to Recoup Loss
10%	11.11%
20%	25.00%
30%	42.85%
40%	66.66%
50%	100%
60%	150%
70%	233%
80%	400%
90%	900%
100%	broke

Notice that as losses (drawdown) increase, the percent gain necessary to recover to breakeven increases at a much faster rate.

FIGURE 1.1

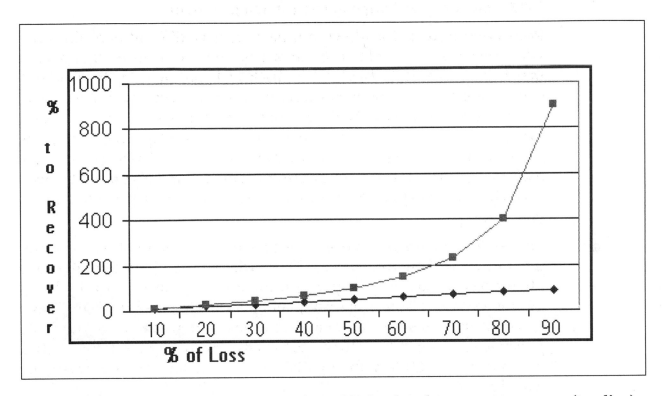

Percent loss (drawdown) vs. percent to recover. Notice that the percent to recover (top line) grows at a geometric rate as the percent loss increases. This illustrates the difficulty of recovering from a loss and why money management is so important.

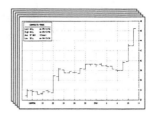

CHAPTER **2**

LANDRY'S RULES AND MONEY MANAGEMENT FOR THE SWING TRADER

1. **Treat Trading as a Business**—Most people wouldn't dream of starting a business without everything necessary. Yet, many, while trying to become a successful trader, cut corners when it comes to equipment. Make sure you create an infrastructure which supports your business on an ongoing and emergency basis. This includes buying the best computers, data and charts you can afford.

2. **Do Your Homework**—In trading you are competing against some of brightest minds in the world. Therefore, you must be willing to put in the necessary hours to be prepared.

3. **Manage Yourself**—In trading you are responsible for all of your decisions. Make sure you are making them with a clear mind. Don't trade if you are sick, distracted, during major life events or if you are simply not prepared.

4. **The Trend *Is* Your Friend**—Market moves often last much longer and go much further than most are willing to admit. Trying to pick tops and bottoms is a loser's game.

5. **Limit Losses**—As soon as a position is initiated, you should have a protective stop right below the recent support (for longs), or above recent resistance (for shorts). For purposes of the setups outlined in the manual, this will usually be below the lowest bar of the setup (for longs) or the highest bar of the setup (for shorts). If this is greater than 5% of the stock's value, risk no more than 5%.

Swing trading often produces many small gains with only an occasional home run. Therefore, protective stops must be used on all trades. Getting careless on just one trade can erase many winners.

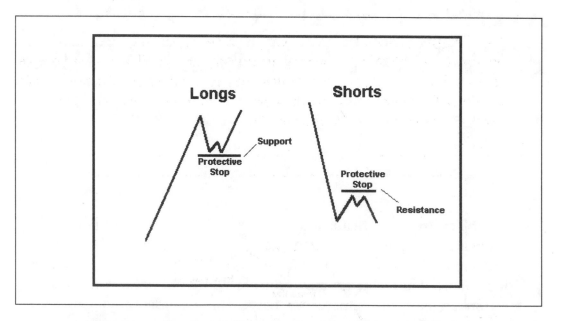

6. **No Tickie, No Tradie**—Swing trading involves identifying short-term support and resistance and where a market will *likely* re-assert itself. **It is *not* about fading the market by picking tops and bottoms.** Therefore, wait for follow through before attempting to enter a trade.

For instance, suppose a market is in rally mode and begins to sell off, chances are the next move will be a resumption of the original uptrend. However, until that uptrend begins to resume, positions should not be initiated. For longs, this means waiting for the market to turn back up, and for shorts, it means waiting for the market to turn back down.

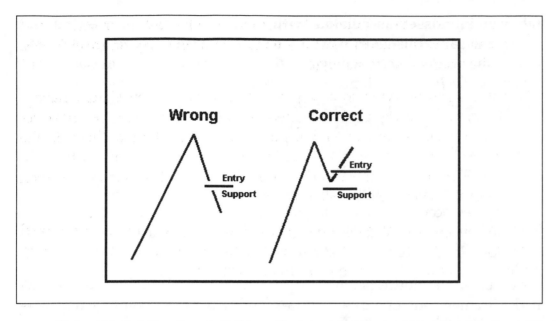

7. **Take Partial Profits Quickly**—On most swing trades, the profits will be small and have the potential to quickly erode. *Therefore, as soon as your profits (a) are equal to or greater than your initial risk (b), you should lock in half of your profits and move your protective stop on your remaining shares to breakeven (c) (near your original entry).*

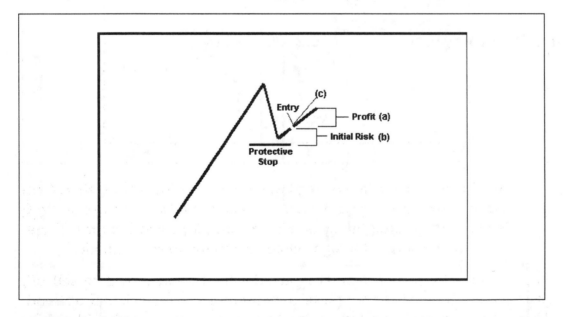

Locking in half of your profits and moving your stop to breakeven when your profits are greater than or equal to your initial risk, will help to generate income for your account. This income will help to pay for the inevitable small losses associated with swing trading. Further, barring overnight gaps, this gives you, at worst, a breakeven trade and a chance at a home run on the remaining position. Larry Connors, in *Connors On Advanced Trading*, has dubbed this simple, yet effective, form of money management "2-for-1 Money Management." We will walk through several examples of this concept under Chapter 15, "More Examples."

8. **Take Windfall Profits**—As a swing trader, windfall profits are often few and far between. Therefore, you should lock in all or a significant piece of your profits when parabolic moves occur. After all, large moves occur as players dog pile onto a market as it becomes obvious to the masses. You've got to ask yourself, once it's obvious and the last players are entering the market, who's left to buy?

As an example, notice below in Figure 2.1 that Agilent Technologies (A) had a tremendous one-day gain (a), but all of those gains were eroded over the next few days (b).

FIGURE 2.1

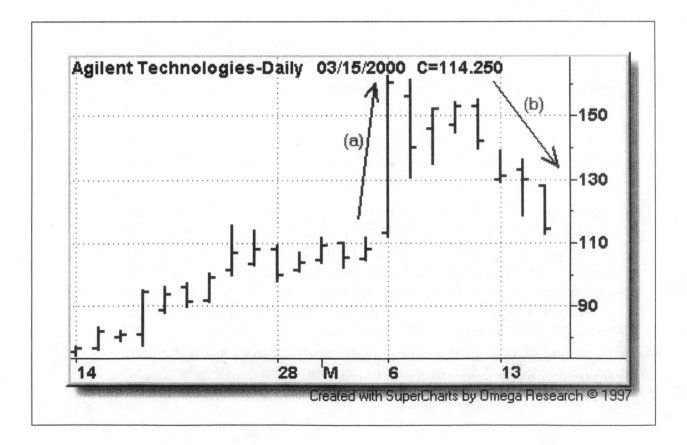

Never, never, never allow the above to happen to you. Not only is this financially debilitating but its also psychologically debilitating.

9. **Trade in Liquid and Active Markets**—As swing traders, we are looking for an immediate short-term move. We don't have the luxury of waiting around until a large price-move takes place. Therefore, the markets we trade in must be liquid and active so we can move in and out with ease, and, hopefully, capture short-term fluctuations. Trading in thin and dull markets can be costly and will likely chew you up, as most short-term trading profits are small. We'll expand upon this concept in Chapter 4, Stock Selection and Section Three, Volatility.

10. **Stack the Odds in Your Favor**—In trading, the more pieces of the puzzle that fit together, the better. This means determining an overall market bias (if any), trading the strongest stocks in the strongest sectors (or weakest stocks in the weakest sectors for shorts) and combining bigger picture technical patterns and studying the volatility of the stock. We'll expand upon these concepts throughout this manual.

11. **Keep Position Size Within Reason**—Swing trading is a game of probabilities. You win some, you lose some, and hopefully, through a consistent approach, you make money overall. Swing trading is not about trying to hit "home runs" by taking excessive risk on any one position. In fact, you should never take a position large enough to have a material impact on your trading account should—or more likely, when—a price shock occurs. In general, you should not risk more than 2% of your account value on any given trade.

12. **Never Add to a Losing Position!**—If you are wrong, then admit it and move on. Averaging down, that is, adding to losing positions is a loser's game.

13. **Enter the Entire Position at Once**—In swing trading we are in the market for a short period of time and looking for a swift move. Unlike the longer-term player who has the luxury of building positions over time and at an average price while waiting for the market to move, the swing trader is looking for an immediate move. In most cases, you should be looking to lock in profits and tighten stops as the market moves in your favor—not add to positions.

    If you must pyramid, then do it quickly as the position moves in your favor, and make sure it looks like an actual pyramid. In other words, only add to profitable positions and establish your largest position first. A 3-2-1 is good ratio for establishing positions. For instance, if your position size is 500 shares, then enter 300, then 200, then 100, provided of course, the market is moving in your favor while adding to the position.

14. **Remain Consistent**—Successful traders find a formula and stick to it. Swing trading is no different. You must find an approach that works for you and apply it in a consistent methodical manner. In addition to being consistent in your approach, you must also be consistent in your money-management techniques. This involves keeping position size within reason, using initial protective stops, taking profits and trailing stops.

15. **When In Doubt, Get Out**—In swing trading, we are looking for an immediate short-term move. If the market doesn't move immediately, then there's no need to remain in the market—even if you're not stopped out. The longer you are in a market that is not moving in your favor, the more you are exposing yourself to a potential adverse move. In *most* cases, you're better off exiting the position and waiting for the market to set up again. A good rule-of-thumb here is to exit positions that aren't profitable within one to two days.

16. **Know When to Say When**—Be willing to stop trading and re-evaluate the markets, yourself and your methodologies when you encounter a string of losses. The markets will always be there. Gann said it best: *"When you make one to three trades that show losses, whether they be large or small, something is wrong with you and not the market. Your trend may have changed. My rule is to get out and wait. Study the reason for your losses. Remember, you will never lose any money by being out of the market."*

17. **Re-Read Rule #5!**

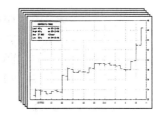

CHAPTER **3**

TREND QUALIFIERS

▪ ▫ ▪ ▫ ▪ ▫ ▪ ▫ ▪ ▫ ▪ ▫ ▪ ▫ ▪ ▫ ▪ ▫ ▪ ▫ ▪ ▫ ▪ ▫ ▪ ▫ ▪

The trend is your friend.

— truest market adage

Most of the methods in this manual involve first identifying strongly trending markets. In this chapter we will look at how to define a trend.

WHAT IS A TREND?

Quite simply an uptrend is a series of higher prices over time. If a stock was at $50 per share a month ago and is now trading at $100 per share, it's obviously in an uptrend. When looking at a bar chart, it is a series of higher highs and higher lows.

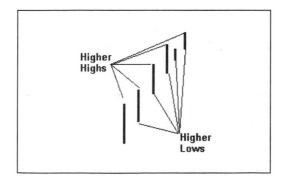

A downtrend is quite simply a series of lower prices over time. If a stock was trading at $100 per share a month ago and is now trading at $50 per share, then obviously it is in a downtrend. When looking at a bar chart, it is a series of lower highs and lower lows.

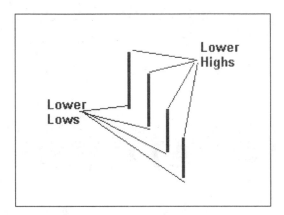

MEASURING TREND

ADX

Developed by Welles Wilder, the ADX is used to measure the strength of a market but not its direction. The higher the reading, the stronger the trend, regardless of whether it is up or down. The direction of the market is suggested by two components that make up the ADX: the Positive Directional Movement Index (+DMI) and the Minus Directional Movement Index (–DMI). In general, an ADX reading of 30 or higher with +DMI > –DMI denotes a strong uptrend. Referring to Figure 3.1 of Veritas Software, notice at point (a) the ADX reading was greater than 30 and the +DMI was above the –DMI suggesting an uptrend was developing.

FIGURE 3.1

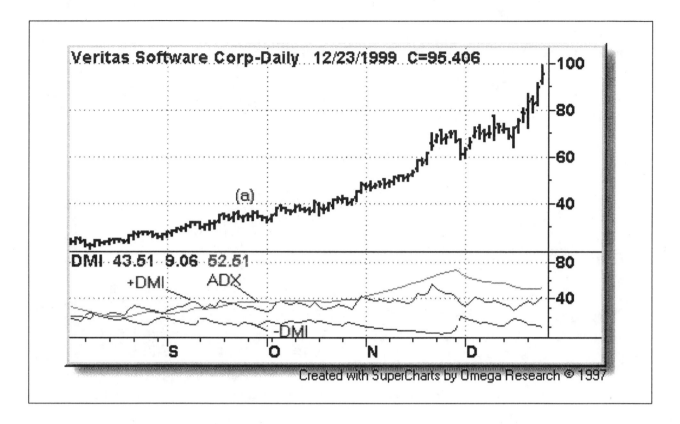

Conversely, an ADX reading of 30 or higher with –DMI > +DMI denotes a strong downtrend. Referring to Figure 3.2 of Metricom, notice that at point (a) the ADX was greater than 30 and the –DMI > +DMI suggesting a strong downtrend was developing.

FIGURE 3.2

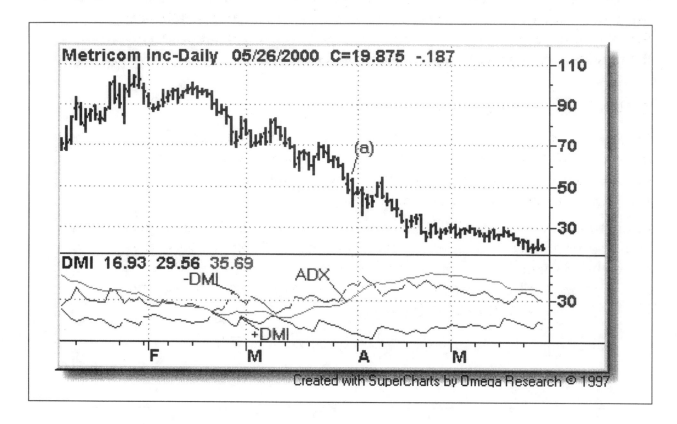

Details on how ADX and DMI are calculated are provided in the Appendix. For purposes of this manual, all you need to know is that ADX >= 30 and +DMI > –DMI suggests an uptrend and ADX >= 30 and –DMI > +DMI suggests a downtrend.

DEVELOPING AN EYE FOR TREND

Many are obsessed with finding exact formulas to define trend. They get caught up in precise measurements. For instance, they won't trade a market because the ADX is less than X or the RS isn't greater than Y. The truth is, like trading in general, there are no "exacts" when it comes to measuring trend.

This is not to say that trend indicators such as ADX do not have their place. These standardized indicators are very useful when running computer scans on thousands of stocks. In addition, to those newer to trading, these indicators can help take away some of the guesswork.

So how should trends be measured? The good news is that determining trend does not have to be complex. With a little experience, you'll find that a simple "eyeballing" of a chart will give you a much better idea of the trend than any precise computerized method.

TREND QUALIFIERS

There are certain clues that a trending market will leave behind. I have dubbed these "Trend Qualifiers." With a little practice, you'll be able to quickly glance at a chart, recognize these patterns and know instinctively whether or not a market is in a strong trend.

Base Breakouts—A base breakout is when a wide-range bar that goes higher occurs after a sideways market movement. When a stock goes sideways, it suggests the buyers and the sellers agree on price. When the stock breaks out of this base, the buyers have gained control with the likelihood that the trend is developing.

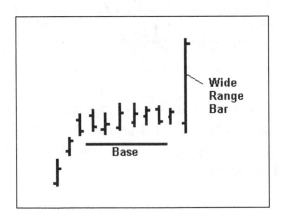

Gaps in the direction of the trend—A gap occurs when a stock opens above the prior day's high (a gap higher) or opens below the prior day's low (a gap lower). When a stock gaps in the direction of the uptrend, it suggests strong demand for the stock as buyers are bidding up the stock before it opens. Note in the diagram below that the lows of the gap days are also greater than the prior day's high. This indicates even more strength.

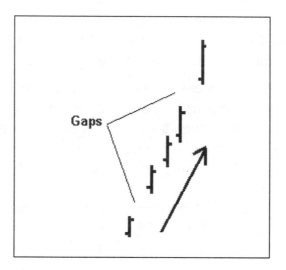

Laps in the direction of the trend—A lap occurs when a stock opens greater than the prior day's close but less than the prior day's high. While not as strong as a gap, a lap in the direction of trend suggests demand for the stock.

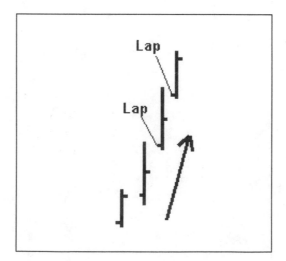

New Highs—A stock must hit new highs if it is in an uptrend. A two-month calendar high (approximately 43 trading days) is a good rule of thumb to use here.

New Lows—A stock must hit new lows if it is in a downtrend. A two-month calendar low (approximately 43 trading days) is a good rule of thumb to use here.

Percentage Moves—how much a stock has risen or fallen over a given period of time. For instance, a stock that goes from $50 to $100 in a month is up 100%. Obviously, though, it doesn't take mathematics Ph.D. to determine that stocks making such moves are in uptrends.

Strong Closes—When a stock closes within the top 25% of its range, it suggests that traders were willing to carry the position overnight. This implies demand for the stock. The more days in a row that this occurs, the stronger the uptrend.

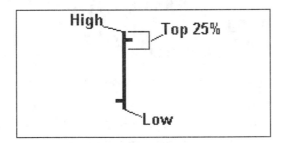

Wide-Range Bars (Thrusts) in the direction of the trend—The stock's range is greater than the prior five days (or more) range.

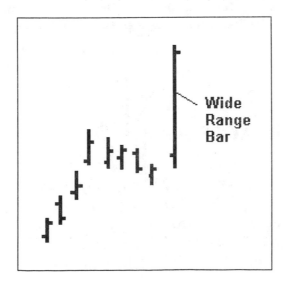

Here's an example of a stock that shows multiple Trend Qualifiers throughout a 90-day period. The trend was easily determined early on by the base breakout. The stock then proceeded to show strong trending characteristics.

FIGURE 3.3

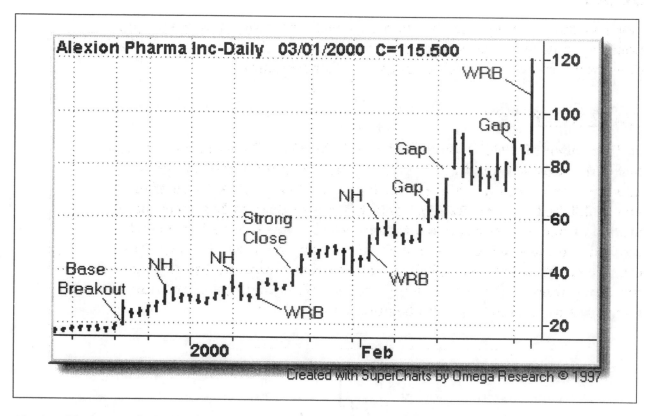

Alexion Pharmaceuticals (ALXN) rises over 700% in 10 weeks. During that period, it broke out from a base, made new two-month highs (NH), had strong closes and gaps and wide-range bars (WRB) in the direction of the uptrend.

MOVING AVERAGES

Moving averages are also helpful when determining trend. I like to use a 10-day simple moving average (SMA), 20-day exponential moving average (EMA) and 30-day EMA. The 10-day SMA gives me a *true* representation of price over the last two weeks (10 trading days). The 20- and 30-period EMAs give a rough representation of performance over the last month and six weeks, respectively. I like the exponential averages for these longer periods as they are front-weighted and catch up to prices faster.

The characteristics of moving averages that I use to help me determine trend include slope, Daylight and proper order.

SLOPE

Slope is quite simply the direction in which the moving averages are pointing. Positive slope suggests an uptrend, negative slope suggests a downtrend and very little slope suggests a consolidation.

DAYLIGHT

In December of 1996, I published the 2/20 EMA Breakout System in *Stocks And Commodities Magazine*. The system essentially looks to go long after two or more lows are greater than the 20-day EMA. Soon after it was published, several traders contacted me to discuss how they used and modified the system to fit their needs. One trader, Joe Sansolo, dubbed the lows being greater than the moving average "Daylight" because you could see "daylight" in between the low of the bar (or highs for downtrends) and the moving average. This daylight many times means the trend is in place and beginning to accelerate.

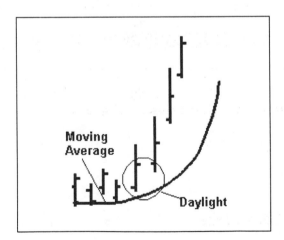

PROPER ORDER

In an uptrend, a faster (shorter time frames) moving average will follow closer to price than a slower (longer time frames) moving average. There-fore, when using a 10-day SMA, a 20-day EMA and a 30-day EMA, the

10-day SMA should be greater than the 20-day EMA and the 20-day EMA should be greater than the 30-day EMA.

Notice the moving averages in Alexion Pharmaceuticals, mentioned previously. There was Daylight and the moving averages were in proper order and had a positive slope throughout its strong uptrend.

FIGURE 3.4

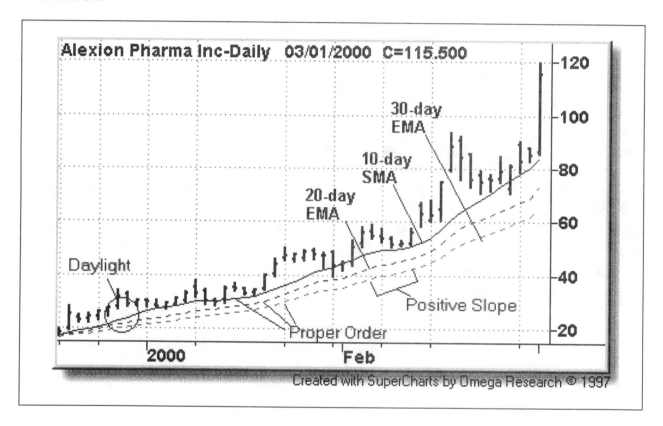

THE TREND SHOULD BE OBVIOUS

Even though we have gone to great length to describe trend, the truth is, it doesn't have to be rocket science. Therefore, don't get too caught up in the specific details. In fact, if you have a young child at home, ask him or her what direction they think a chart is headed. If you don't have any young kids, think to yourself, "In which direction would a 6-year-old say this stock is headed?"

And finally, keep in mind that markets only trend about 30% of the time. Trade that 30% and ignore the remaining 70%. This will further ensure you are trading in the correct markets.

Q&A

Q. Do you recommend any additional reading on determining trends?

A. Yes. Mark Boucher has done intensive studies of early identification of runaway markets. He has quantified market constructs such as gaps, laps and thrusts. He published this research in his book *The Hedge Fund Edge.*

Q. Are there any hard fast rules when it comes to determining trend?

A. No. If the right side of the chart is higher than the left, then that is an uptrend. If the right side of the chart is lower than the left side, then it is in a downtrend. Seriously, it should be obvious.

Q. You used 10-day simple and 20-day and 30-day exponential moving averages for stocks. Do you also use these in other markets?

A. Yes. For an index, like the Nasdaq or S&P, I like to also plot a 50-day and 200-day simple moving average simply because it is well-watched by institutions.

Q. Is a simple moving average better than an exponential moving average or vise versa?

A. I think both have their place. I like the simple for shorter time periods, say 10 days or less, because this gives me true representation of the average price. Longer term, I like to use exponential moving averages as they still give me a feel for the longer-term average price, but being front-weighted, tend to catch up to current prices faster.

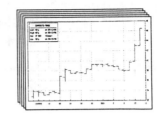

CHAPTER **4**

STOCK SELECTION

▫ ▫

As momentum swing traders, we are looking to capture explosive short-term market moves. We do not have the luxury of waiting around for something to happen. Therefore, it's vitally important that we are trading in stocks that show the most immediate potential. Obviously, as momentum players, trend is one of our main criteria. In addition to trend, the stocks must be volatile, a member of the strongest sector, priced high enough and have a reasonable spread to make short-term trading worthwhile. These, along with several other criteria for selecting stocks, are discussed below.

Trend—In general, the stocks should have an ADX reading of 30 or higher and +DMI > –DMI for uptrends and –DMI > +DMI for downtrends. Keep in mind that no indicator guarantees that a stock is in a trend. Therefore, make sure the trend is obvious (regardless of the ADX reading) and shows characteristics described under "Trend Qualifiers."

Sector—Trade in stocks that are members of the strongest sectors. The old stock market adage "A rising tide lifts all boats" is as relevant to individual sectors as it is to the major averages. In fact, because sectors can often outperform and even trade counter to the overall market, the sector action is more important than the overall stock market.

Under ideal conditions, the overall sector should be in a strong trend. However, keep in mind that sometimes sub-sectors can trade independently of the overall sector. For instance, in mid-2000, the telecommunication stocks overall were in a strong downtrend but the fiber sub-sector was in a strong uptrend.

Spread—The spread is the difference between the bid price and the ask price. For instance, if a stock is bidding 98 and asking 100, it has a 2-point spread. So if you bought that stock at the market for $100, you would immediately have a 2-point loss, as the best you could sell the stock for would be $98. In general, you should avoid stocks with such large spreads and focus on issues that have a spread of ½ point or less. Keep in mind, however, that in trading, there are trade-offs. Sometimes stocks in fast moves will have larger spreads, as traders are reluctant to sell near the bid. In these cases, you'll have to decide whether or not the potential for gains outweighs the immediate loss.

Price—As I've learned from Jeff Cooper, professional trader and author of *Hit and Run Trading I & II*, if you are going to trade on a short-term basis, you need to be in higher-priced stocks. This is because they have the potential to make larger *point* moves than their lower-priced counterparts. For instance, a $10 stock must gain 30% in value for a 3-point move. A $50 stock would only have to gain 6% and $100 stock would only have to gain 3%. Therefore, I suggest only trading in stocks priced $20 and preferable $30 or higher.

Price Persistency—Focus on those stocks that tend to be most price persistent. This means that the stock price tends to follow through from one day to the next. For instance, if the stock is up sharply today, it tends to follow through to the upside over the next few days. I have yet to find an accurate measurement of persistency other than looking at charts. Notice how a stock acts when coming out of a pullback. Does it tend to thrust and fail? Or do thrusts tend to carry through over the next few days?

Daily Range—The stock must exhibit the potential to make large moves over a short period of time. One of the easiest ways to recognize this potential is to look at the average range (high – low). As a general rule, the average range should be two points or higher.

Volume/Liquidity—One advantage of being a smaller independent trader versus an institution is that you can trade in smaller cap issues. Many times, these issues have the potential to make larger gains than their bigger cap counterparts. However, the issues need to be liquid enough to allow you to move in and out with ease. In general, the stock's 10-day average volume should be at least 100,000 shares.

Volatility—Volatility is simply how much prices fluctuate over time. The longer-term trader has the luxury of waiting for a stock to move. The swing trader, on the other hand, is looking for an immediate move within a short time frame. Therefore, he must trade in more volatile issues. I believe the best, standardized measurement of volatility is historical volatility (HV). Stocks you trade should have a HV reading of at least 40% or higher. I will discuss HV in further detail in Section Three, Volatility.

CHAPTER **5**

PULLBACKS

▫ ▫

The simplest theory that fits the facts of a problem
is the one that should be selected.

— Occam's Razor

Although I emphasize trading with the trend, this does **not** mean blindly buying a stock simply because it is in a strong uptrend. Strongly trending markets are prone to correct. And, you never know when what appears to be a correction, may in fact be the end of the trend. Therefore, it's much wiser to wait for the correction to occur and then look to enter if (*and only if*) the original trend begins to re-assert itself—this is the theory and essence of the pullback. **In my opinion, this is the single strongest way to trade.**

Referring to Figure 5.1, a hypothetical pullback example, the market is in a strong uptrend (a) and begins to correct (b). Upon trend resumption (a rally), an entry is triggered (c). A protective stop (d) is placed right below the low of the pullback (d), just in case the correction is not complete.

FIGURE 5.1

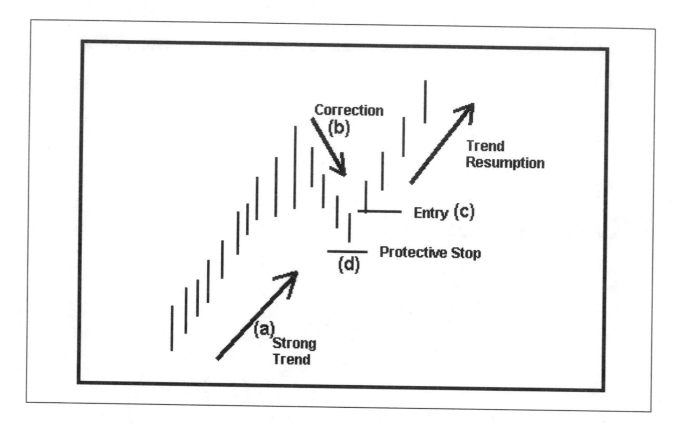

Entering if, *and only if*, the trend resumes helps to avoid markets that have topped. Notice in Figure 5.2, another hypothetical example, what at first looked like a pullback, turned out to be the exact top of the market and the beginning of a new downtrend.

FIGURE 5.2

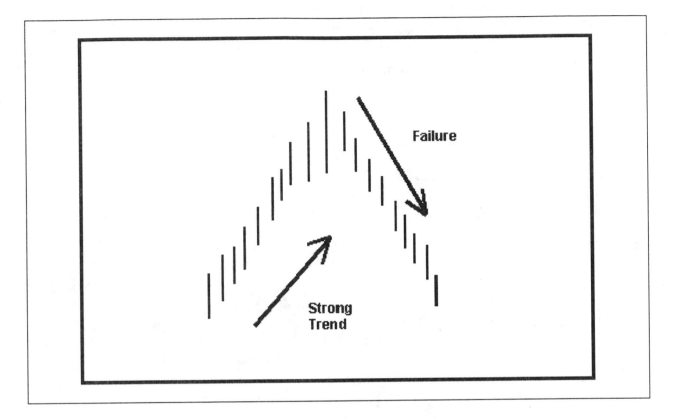

Trends often last much longer and go much further than most are willing to accept. Markets often thrust, pull back and thrust over and over again. This is why top and bottom picking is often a loser's game.

This is *not* to say that trends last forever. Eventually, all trends end. Therefore, when trading pullbacks, there's always a chance that what appears to be yet another pullback, in fact, turns out to be a major reversal. However, by waiting for an entry and using protective stops, you may be fortunate enough to either avoid the trade (no entry) or get stopped out with no more than a modest loss.

Infospace (INSP) provides a good real-world example. Referring to Figure 5.3, notice that the stock "stair stepped" higher, over and over again, but eventually fails. One note of observation: The more times a stock pulls back and resumes its trend, the less likely the next pullback will follow through. Said another way, early pullbacks are superior to later pullbacks.

FIGURE 5.3

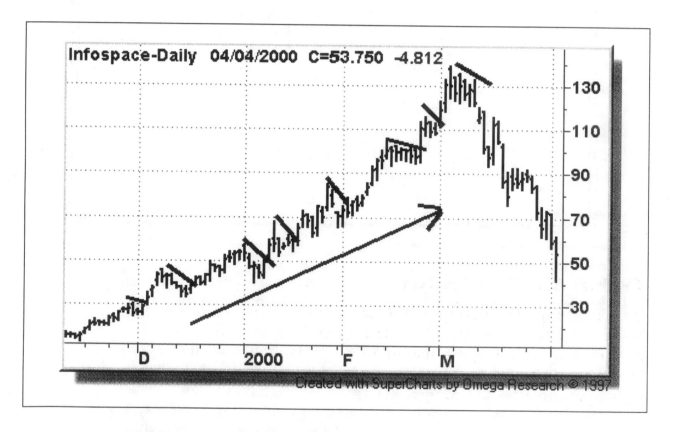

Infospace-Daily 04/04/2000 C=53.750 -4.812

DEFINING A PULLBACK

A pullback can be defined in terms of the trend, the new high, the width and the depth. These are illustrated in Figure 5.4.

FIGURE 5.4

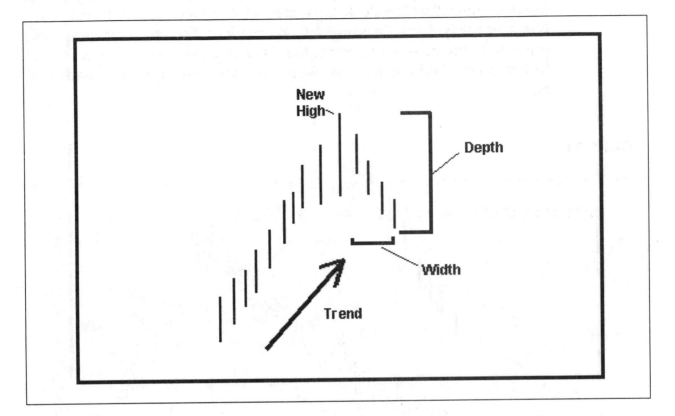

TREND AND NEW HIGH

Obviously, a market must be in a trend and make a significant new high before a pullback can take place. Trend can be defined in terms of an ADX reading of 30 or higher and +DMI > –DMI or by other Trend Qualifiers (Chapter 3). The new high should be at least a two-month calendar high (approximately 43 trading days).

WIDTH

The width is the number of bars since the last new high was made. For instance, a four-bar pullback has gone four days since its last new high. This is illustrated in Figure 5.5.

FIGURE 5.5

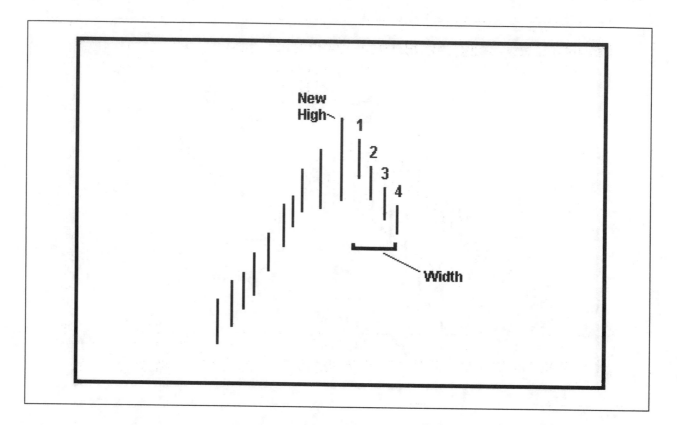

The width should be wide enough so the market has enough time to correct but not too long as to negate the market's initial momentum. Three-to-seven bars is a good rule of thumb here. Referring to Figure 5.6, Emulex (EMLX), notice that after pulling back for eight days (a), the stock begins to drift sideways (b).

FIGURE 5.6

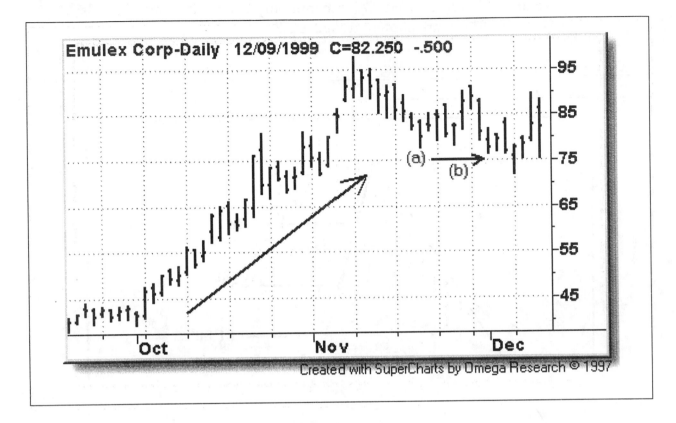

DEPTH

Depth is how much the market gives up during the correction. For instance, if a stock rallies up to 100 (a new high) and then sells off to 90, then it has pulled back 10% off its highs.

Shallow pullbacks tend to lead to longer-term, smoother continuation moves. Deeper pullbacks tend to lead to much shorter-term and much sharper "knee-jerk" reactions. In general, I consider pullbacks of 15% or less shallow and those greater than 15% deep. Keep in mind that "shallow" and "deep" become *somewhat* arbitrary and depend on the volatility of the stock.

RETRACEMENTS

Depth can also be measured in terms of how much of the underlying trend has been retraced. For instance, if a stock rallies 20 points since its last significant low and then gives up 2 points, that stock has retraced 10% of its prior trend. Referring to Figure 5.7, notice that if a stock rallies from (a) to (b) and then drops all the way back to (c), then 100% of that trend has been retraced. Other commonly used retracement levels: 38.2%, 50% and 61.8% are shown in Figure 5.7.

FIGURE 5.7

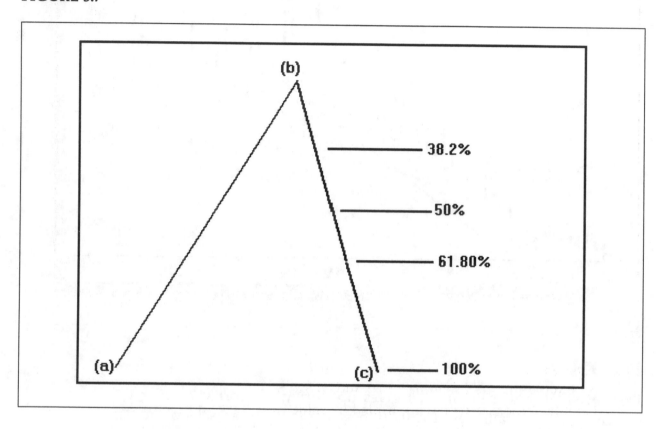

Let's look at some examples of pullbacks.

Here we have an example of a three-bar pullback.

FIGURE 5.8

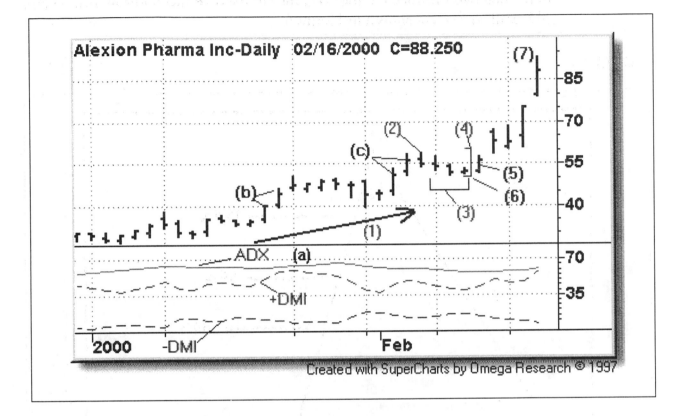

1. Alexion Pharmaceuticals (ALXN) qualifies as a strongly trending stock by having an ADX reading of 60 and +DMI > –DMI (a). Other Trend Qualifiers include its having tripled in value over the two months and wide-range bars (b) and strong closes (c) in the direction of the uptrend.

2. The stock makes a new two-month high.

3. It pulls back three bars (width).

4. This is 13% off the prior new high (depth) creating a fairly shallow pullback. This suggests that the stock has the potential to make a longer-term continuation move. Go long tomorrow at 53 1/16, 1/16 above today's high.

5. The trend resumes as the stock trades at 53 1/16, 1/16 above the prior day's high and we go long.

6. A protective stop is placed at 50 15/16, 1/16 below the lowest bar in the pullback.

7. After a slow start, the stock skyrockets over 40 points over the next five days.

Here's an example on the short side.

FIGURE 5.9

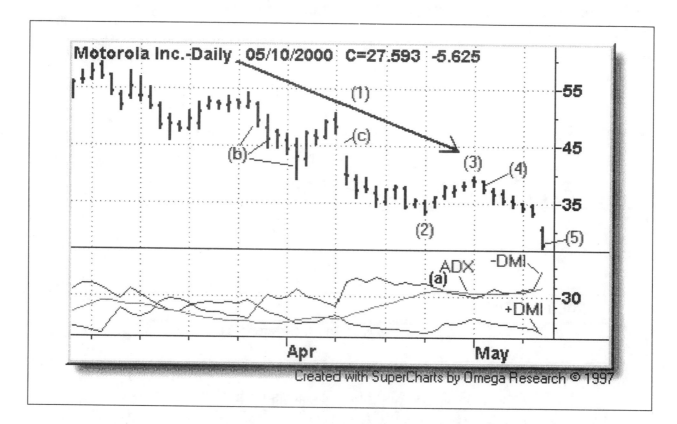

1. Motorola (MOT) qualifies as being in a downtrend by having an ADX reading of 32 and –DMI > +DMI (a). Other Trend Qualifiers include its having lost over 40% of its value in less than two months and its having wide-range bars lower (b) and a gap in the direction of the downtrend (c).

2. The stock makes a two-month low.

3. The stock pulls back 17.9% (depth) in five bars (width). Go short tomorrow at 38 1/16, 1/16 below today's low.

4. The stock trades at 38 1/16 and we go short. A protective stop is placed at 39 5/8, 1/16 above the highest bar in the pullback (3).

5. The downward trend resumes as the stock drops over ten points over the next seven days.

An easy way to recognize or scan for pullbacks is to look for three to seven consecutive *lower* highs after a stock hits a new high. I have dubbed these "Simple Pullbacks." These often set up as pullbacks described by Gann over 65 years ago and extensions of his work such as Connors'/Cooper's 1-2-3-4s.

After at least three, but no more than seven lower highs, look to go long tomorrow if the stock can trade 1/16 above today's high.

FIGURE 5.10

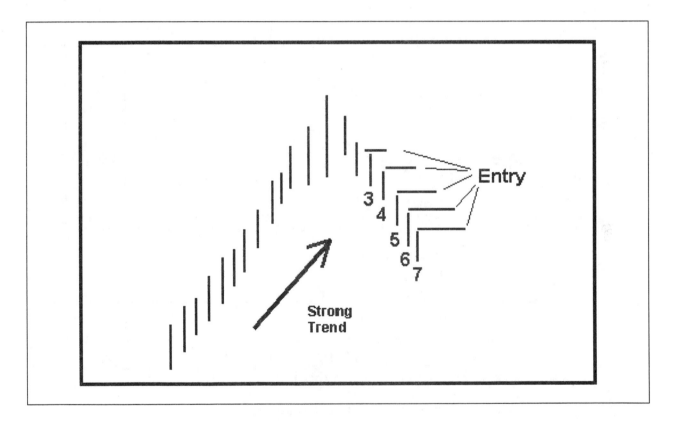

Here's an example of a four-bar "Simple" pullback.

FIGURE 5.11

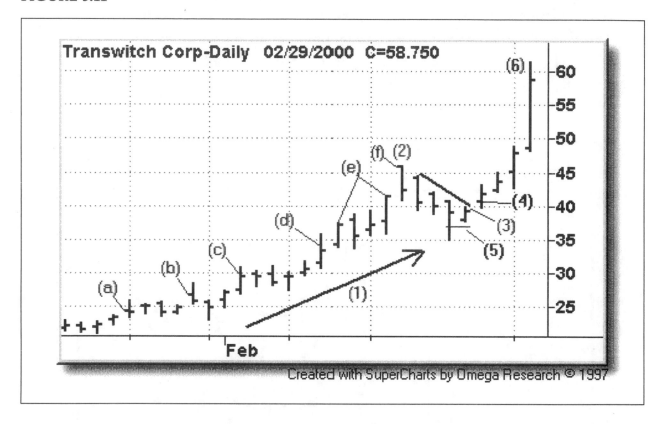

1. Transwitch (TXCC) qualifies as a strongly trending stock by having an ADX of 46 and +DMI > –DMI (not shown). In addition, other trend Qualifiers include its rising over 200% in less than a month and its having gaps (a), (b) and (f), and its having wide-range bars, (d) and (e), and strong closes (e) in the direction of the uptrend.

2. The stock makes a new two-month high.

3. The stock makes four consecutive lower highs. Go long tomorrow at 39 3/4, 1/16 above today's high.

4. The stock gaps open to 40 11/16 (above our entry) and we go long.

5. Because the low of the formation (35 3/16) is more than 13% away from our entry, we will only risk 5% of the stock's value and place a protective stop at 38 5/8.

6. The stock resumes its uptrend and trades around 18 points higher over the four days.

I have observed that deeper pullbacks, say 15% or greater, of stocks in strong trends tend to create a "knee-jerk" reaction. This is based on the fact that when a stock pulls back sharply, it creates an out-of-balance situation, as eager shorts jump into the market and nervous longs bail out.

Like a rubber band being stretched to extremes, the market often violently "snaps back" in the direction of the longer-term trend as shorts scramble to cover and longs jump back in. Therefore, I have dubbed deep pullbacks "Snapbacks."

FIGURE 5.12

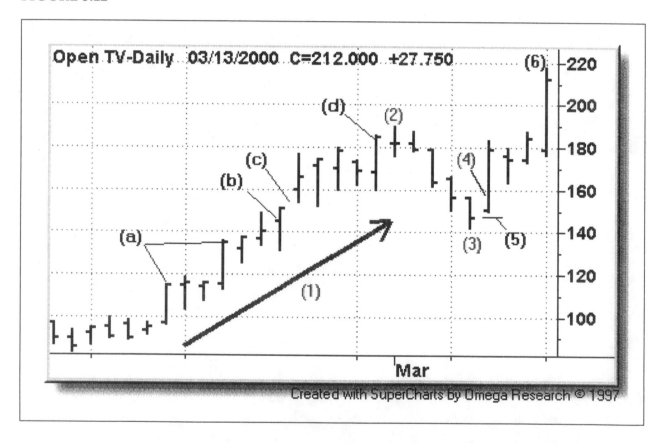

1. Open TV (OPTV) qualifies as a strongly trending stock by having an ADX reading of 49 and +DMI > –DMI (not shown). In addition, other Trend Qualifiers include its more than doubling in less than a month, its having wide-range bars with strong closes, (a) and (d), and a lap (b) and a gap (c) in the direction of the uptrend.

2. Open TV makes a new two-month high.

3. The stock has a sharp 25% sell-off (depth) over four days (width). Buy tomorrow at 156 1/16, 1/16 above today's high.

4. The stock trades through at 156 1/16 and we go long.

5. Because the low of the setup (3) is more than 8% away from out entry, we will risk 5% of the stocks value and place an initial protective stop at 148 1/4.

6. The stock explodes out of the deep pullback and trades over 60 points higher over the next four days.

Here's another example of a deep pullback or a "Snapback."

FIGURE 5.13

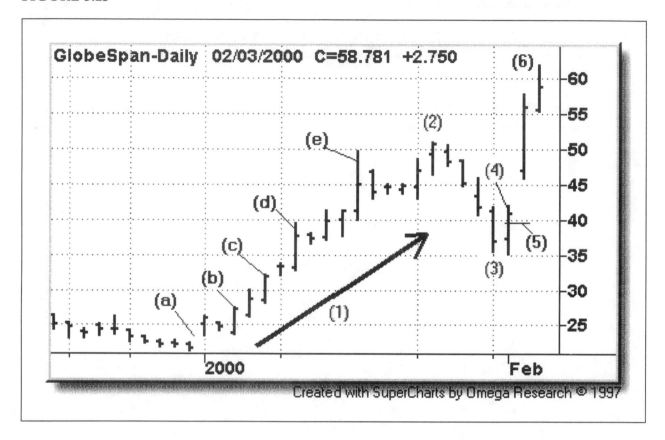

1. GlobeSpan (GSPN) qualifies as a strongly trending stock by having an ADX reading of 50 and +DMI > –DMI (not shown). In addition, other Trend Qualifiers include its more than doubling in less than a month, and its having a gap (a), wide-range bars (b), (c), (d) and (e), and strong closes (b), (c) and (d) in the direction of the uptrend.

2. GlobeSpan makes a new two-month high.

3. The stock has a sharp 30% sell-off (depth) over four days (width). Go long tomorrow at 41 3/4, 1/16 above today's high.

4. The stock trades at 41 3/4 and we go long.

5. Because the bottom of the formation (3) is more than 14% away from our entry, we set an initial protective stop 5% below our entry at 39 5/8.

6. The strong uptrend resumes and the stock trades over 50% higher the
    next two days.

Here's an example of a deep pullback (Snapback) of a stock with a low ADX but still in a downtrend.

FIGURE 5.14

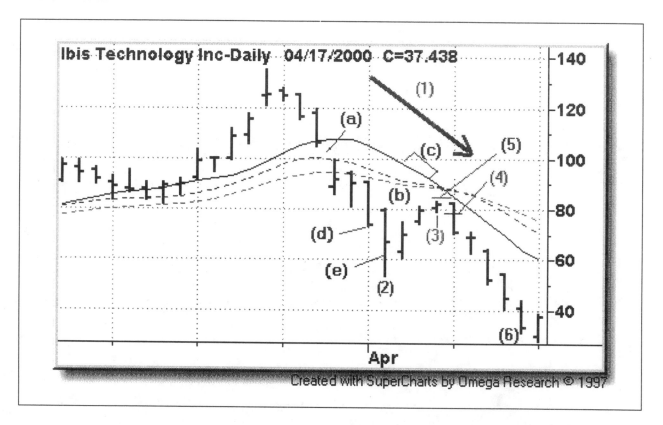

1. Ibis Technology (IBIS) has a fairly low ADX reading of 27 (not shown) but obviously is in a downtrend after losing 60% of its value (high to low) in less than two weeks. Other Trend Qualifiers include its having a gap lower (a), Daylight (highs less than the moving averages) (b), negative slope in the 10-day simple, 20-day exponential and 30-day exponential moving averages (c), a poor close on a wide-range bar lower (d) and another wide-range bar lower (e).

2. The stock makes a new two-month low.

3. The stock has a sharp 35% rally (depth) over three days (width). Go short tomorrow at 79 7/16, 1/16 below today's low.

4. The stock trades at 79 7/16 and we go short.

5. An initial protective stop is placed at 82 7/8, 1/16 above the highest high of the pullback.

6. The stock drops over 40 points over the next four days.

Due to their limited trading history, Initial Public Offerings (IPOs) lend themselves well to the standard 38.2%, 50% and 61.8% retracement levels as the significant "low" and "high" is more obvious than stocks with longer history.

FIGURE 5.15

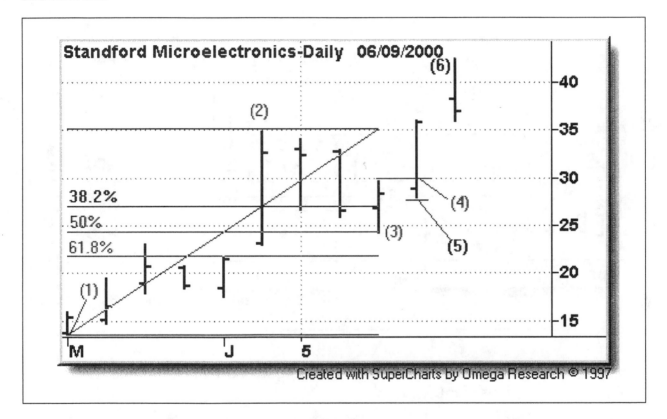

1. Standford Microelectronics (SMDI), an IPO, makes a low on its first day of trading. This is obvious *after* (2).

2. The stock more than doubles over the next week.

3. The stock pulls back 50% of its prior move. Buy tomorrow at 29 11/16, 1/16 above today's high.

4. The stock trades at 29 11/16 and we are long.

5. Because the low of the setup (3) is nearly 18% away, we place an initial protective stop 1 ½ points, approximately 5%, below our entry.

6. The stock rallies more than 15 points over two days.

Here's another example of using retracement levels on IPOs.

FIGURE 5.16

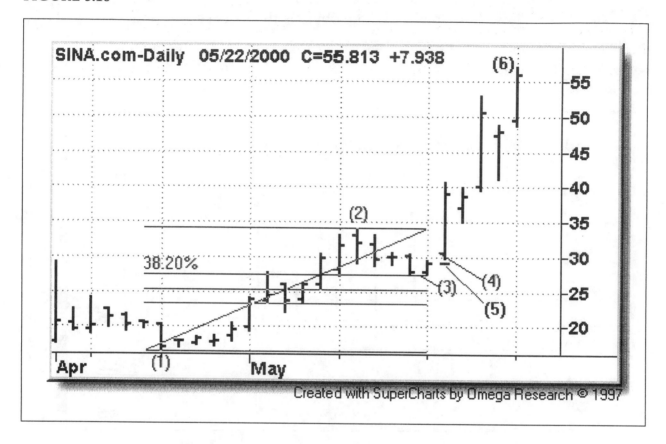

1. SINA.com (SINA) makes a low the second week of trading. This is obvious *after* (2).

2. The stock runs up over 200% over the next 11 days.

3. The stock retraces 38.2%. Go long tomorrow at 29 9/16, 1/16 above today's high.

4. The stock gaps open to 30 7/16 and we go long.

5. Because the low of the setup is more than 8% away from our entry, we place a protective stop at 28 15/16 for a risk of 1 ½ points or 5%.

6. The stock resumes its uptrend and explodes more than 20 points higher over the next five days.

An outside day occurs when a stock trades both below the prior day's low and above the prior day's high. When the price drops below the prior day's low, it attracts sellers. However, if the price reverses and rallies above the prior day's high, buyers are then drawn into the market. This intraday reversal can lead to longer-term reversals. This is especially true when the stock closes strongly—suggesting that the buyers won the battle. When an outside day occurs in a pullback, it suggests that the correction (pullback) is over.

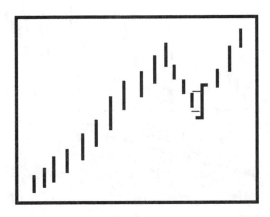

Here's an example of an outside day in a pullback.

FIGURE 5.17

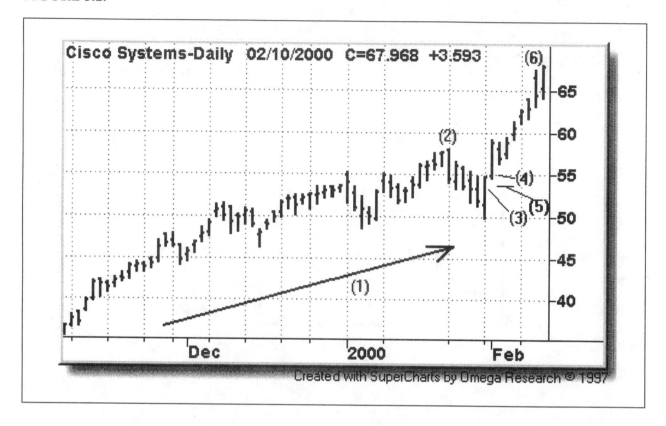

1. Cisco Systems (CSCO) qualifies as a strongly trending stock by having an ADX reading of 30 and +DMI > −DMI (not shown). Other Trend Qualifiers include a steady uptrend where the stock nearly doubles in less than three months.

2. A two-month high.

3. The stock makes four consecutive lower highs then sells off intraday but reverses to close well. This action forms an outside day. Go long tomorrow at 54 7/8, 1/16 above today's high.

4. The stock trades at 54 7/8 and we go long.

5. Because the low of the setup is more than 9% away from our entry, we risk 5% of the stock's value and place an initial protective stop at 52 1/8.

6. The intraday reversal of trend continues and the stock trades over 13 points higher in eight days.

Here's an example an outside day on the short side:

FIGURE 5.18

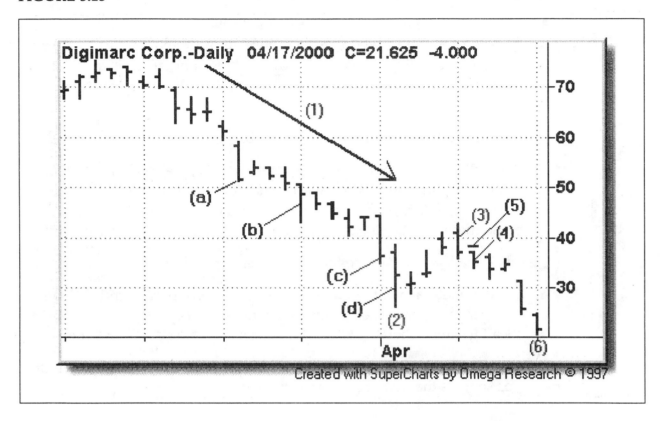

1. Digimarc Corp. (DMRC) qualifies as being a strongly trending stock by having an ADX of 38 and –DMI > +DMI (not shown) and by losing over 70% of its value in less than a month. Other Trend Qualifiers include its having wide-range bars lower (a), (b), (c) and (d), and its having poor closes (a) and (c).

2. A two-month low.

3. An outside day down forms after the stock pulls back three bars. Go short tomorrow at 35 1/16, 1/16 below today's low.

4. The stock trades at 35 15/16 and we go short.

5. Because the high of the formation is more than 18% away from our entry, we will place a protective stop at 37 3/4 for a risk of approximately 5%.

6. The trend continues from the outside day and the stock drops 15 points in five days.

Q&A

Q.   Why do pullbacks work?

A.   First and foremost, you are trading with the trend. Second, you are allowing for the market to have a normal and often healthy correction before attempting an entry. Third, you enter only if the market shows signs of the major trend resuming. Conceptually, this makes a lot of sense.

Q.   Referring to the components of a pullback. How deep is too deep?

A.   A pullback is akin to the "two steps forward one step back" analogy. With that in mind, you have to question a pullback once it retraces more than 50% of the original trend. It also depends upon the stock. The more volatile stocks, by nature, tend to have deeper corrections.

Q.   Is a shallow pullback better than a deeper pullback?

A.   It depends on your trading style. Shallow pullbacks tend to lead to longer term, smoother continuation moves. Deeper pullbacks tend to lead to much shorter term and much sharper "knee-jerk" reactions.

Q.   Why not wait until the old highs are exceeded (b) instead of entering as soon as the trend begins to resume (a)?

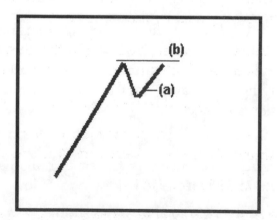

A.   You would miss the move from the pullback entry (a) to the old highs (b). Often, this can be substantial. And, in many cases, this might be all you get.

Q.   Why?

A. Once you get all the way back to the prior new high (b), those who bought at those levels previously may be looking to get out at breakeven.

Q. Hence, a potential double top?

A. Exactly.

Q. Provided you entered during the resumption of the trend (a), would you look to take profits as the old highs are approached?

A. Yes, at this juncture, the market either breaks through or fails. Therefore, you should take partial profits and tighten your stops on the rest of your position. This way if it doesn't break through, at least you made money on your overall position. And if it does, then you have a chance at a home run on your remaining shares.

Q. You discussed that markets often "stair step" higher. How do you know that this stair step won't be the last?

A. You don't. You have to keep playing the stock as if the trend will last forever. Hopefully, you won't get triggered on that last pullback (i.e. a false pullback). Or, at worst, you'll get stopped out with a modest loss. The good news is that markets often offer many opportunities before they eventually fail.

Q. On your retracement examples, you drew lines at 38.2%, 50% and 61.8%. Were these generated by the computer?

A. Yes, but I had to manually pick the low and the high I was measuring. Retracement lines are available in most charting packages.

Q. Back to the levels, why 38.2%, 50% and 61.8%?

A. The 50% level is a logical level, as it is half of the original trend. We're all familiar with the phrase "two steps forward, one step back."

Q. And the 38.2% and 61.8% levels?

A. The 38.2% and 61.8% levels are based on Fibonacci Ratios.

Q. Fibonacci?

A. A Fibonacci sequence is derived by adding a series of numbers together. The sum of each two numbers is added to the prior number. The process is then repeated. For instance, $1 + 1 = 2$, $1 + 2 = 3$, $2 + 3 =$

5 and so forth. So you end up with the sequence: 1,1,2,3,5,8,13,21,34,55,89.... What's interesting is that after about seven iterations, any number in the sequence divided by the prior number = 1.618. Therefore, any prior number is the subsequent number less 38.2% (1 – .618). What's also interesting is that you can start with any two random numbers and these ratios will begin to show up after about seven iterations.

Q.   Is there something magical about these numbers?

A.   The numerologists believe they hold the answer to the universe as these ratios can be found throughout nature. They point out everything from planetary relationships to the level of a women's navel. Others think it was originally just a math exercise developed to teach students how to add.

Q.   Where do you stand?

A.   I always considered them hocus-pocus until I noticed Kevin Haggerty, former head of trading for Fidelity, occasionally showing retracements in his commentary on TradingMarkets.com. I figured if someone of his stature watched these levels then so should I.

Q.   So they *are* magical?

A.   No. I think they have become a self-fulfilling prophecy.

Q.   Anything "watched" is worth watching?

A.   Exactly.

Q.   You mentioned outside days in pullbacks. Hasn't this setup already triggered as a pullback?

A.   Yes, it has. But, you can't watch every single pullback to see if it will trigger. By looking for outside days in pullbacks, you not only catch those that triggered, but triggered from an intraday reversal.

Q.   Does an outside day in a pullback work better if the stock gaps lower (for longs) before reversing to form the outside day?

A.   A gap down would likely scare out more players and when it came back, it would draw them back in. So, yes, a gap lower would probably work as well, if not better.

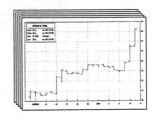

SECTION TWO

MORE SWING TRADING PATTERNS

CHAPTER **6**

FAKEOUTS AND FALSE MOVES

○ ○

We won't get fooled again.

— The Who

Even markets in the strongest trends are prone to shakeout moves and false rallies. These markets may also form false tops that draw in eager shorts and knock out nervous longs.

The following patterns were born out of the frustration of being caught in these shakeout moves, false rallies and false tops. From this I've learned that no matter how strongly a market is trending, I should not enter until *after* some sort of correction has occurred. I've also learned that I shouldn't try to pick a top and that a stock may still be worth trading even if I'm stopped out on my first entry.

TREND KNOCKOUTS

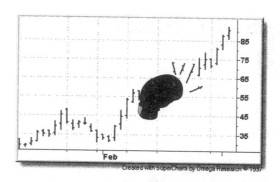

While it's a good idea to trade in the direction of the trend, I've learned you're much better off waiting until the weak hands are knocked out of the market before entering yourself. The reason is, you never know when these traders are going to dump their positions and take you out with them. Trend Knockouts (TKOs) identify strong trends from which the weak hands have already been knocked out. By placing your order above the market, you have the potential to capture profits as the trend resumes.

Here are the rules for Trend Knockouts:

For Buys: (Short Sales are reversed).

1. The market should be in a strong trend as defined by a computer-based indicator such as ADX >= 30 and +DMI > –DMI or as defined under Trend Qualifiers (Chapter 3).

2. The market should make at least a two-bar low. Buy tomorrow or the next day (allow yourself two days to get filled), 1/16 above today's high.

3. Place a protective stop below the low of the knockout bar (2). If this is more than 5% away from your entry, risk no more than 5% of the stock's value.

Let's look at four examples.

FIGURE 6.1

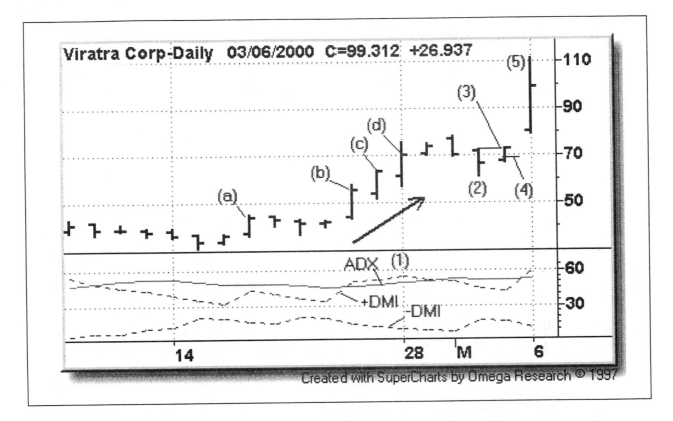

1. Viratra Corp. (VRTA) qualifies as a strongly trending stock by having an ADX of 52 and +DMI > –DMI. Other Trend Qualifiers include its doubling in value in two weeks and having wide-range bars and strong closes in the direction of the trend (a), (b), (c) and (d).

2. The stock sells off and takes out (trades below) the two prior lows. Buy tomorrow at 71 13/16, 1/16 above today's high.

3. The stock trades at 71 13/16 and we go long.

4. Because the low of the setup (61 1/4) is more than 5% away from our entry, we place our protective stop at 63 3/16 for a risk of 5%.

5. The trend resumes as the stock gaps open and explodes over 30 points higher on the following day.

Here we have an example of getting filled on the second day.

FIGURE 6.2

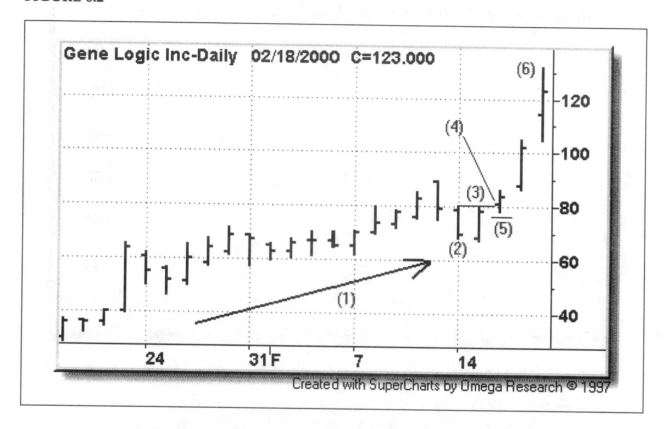

1. Gene Logic (GLGC) qualifies as a strongly trending stock by rising more than 300% in less than a month and by having an ADX of 63 and +DMI > –DMI (not shown).

2. The stock makes a two-bar low. Buy tomorrow at 79 7/8, 1/16 above today's high.

3. No fill.

4. The stock trades at 79 7/8 and we go long.

5. The low of the setup (68) is more than 5% away from our entry so we place a protective stop at 75 7/8 for a risk of 5% of the entry price.

6. The trend resumes and the stock explodes higher over the next few days.

FIGURE 6.3

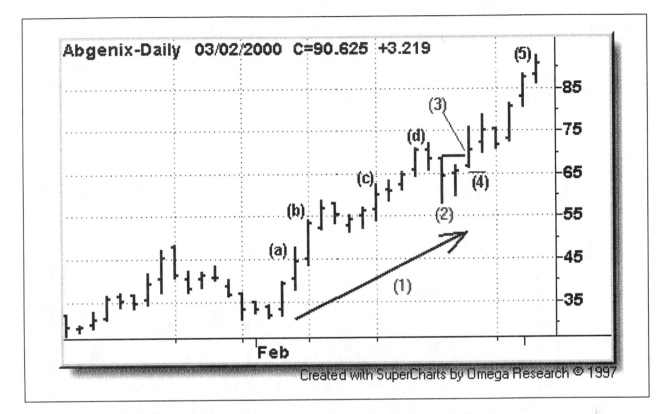

1. Abgenix (ABGX) qualifies as a strongly trending stock by having an ADX of 47 and +DMI > –DMI (not shown). Other Trend Qualifiers include its more than doubling in less than three weeks and having wide-range bars (a), (b), (c) and (d), and its having strong closes in the direction of the uptrend (b) and (d).

2. The stock makes a two-bar low. Buy tomorrow or the next day at 68 9/16, 1/16 above today's high.

3. The stock trades at 68 9/16 and we go long.

4. The low of the formation (57 7/8) is more than 5% away from our entry, so we place a protective stop at 65 1/8 for a risk of 5%.

5. The trend resumes and the stock trades over 20 points higher over the next six days.

Here's another example of Gene Logic (GLGC) but this time, it's on the short side.

FIGURE 6.4

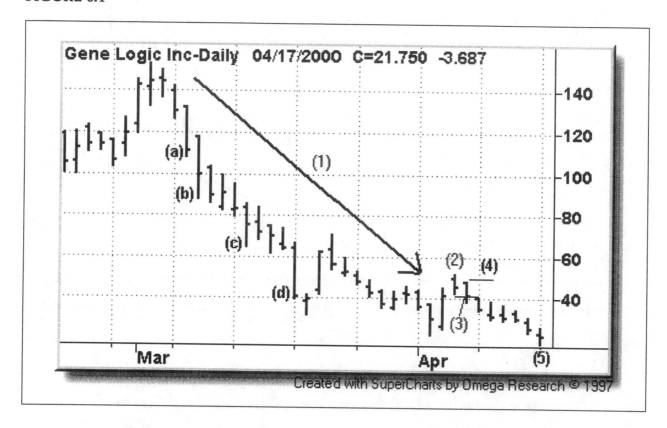

1. Gene Logic qualifies as a strongly trending stock by having an ADX of 31 and –DMI > +DMI (not shown). Other Trend Qualifiers include its losing more than 80% of its value in a month and its having wide-range bars (a), (b), (c) and (d), and weak closes (a) and (d).

2. A two-bar high. Go short tomorrow at 43 7/16, 1/16 below today's low.

3. The stock trades at 43 7/16 and we go short.

4. Because the high of the setup (51 3/4) is more than 5% away from our entry, we place a protective stop at 45 5/8 for a risk of 5%.

5. The downtrend resumes and the stock drops over 24 points in seven days.

Q&A

Q. How did you discover this pattern?

A. Many times, I would get stopped out of positions, only to watch in frustration as the trend resumed.

Q. Why not just re-enter when the trend resumed?

A. I now know that second entries, after being stopped out, are often the best entries but I didn't always know that. Someone once said that a loss is not a loss as long as something is learned from it. I learned TKOs from getting stopped out.

Q. So the loses were painful?

A. Yes. I found it aggravating that I sold stock or futures at a bargain to someone who was now making money. I would eventually "throw in the towel" and jump back into the market, only to get knocked out one more time. I knew I had to come up with a better way to enter strongly trending markets.

Q. The setup calls for "at least" a two-bar low. Does a three-bar low or greater work better?

A. Yes, in general, the more players that are knocked out the better. You are just less likely to get filled.

DOUBLE TOP KNOCKOUT (DT-KO)

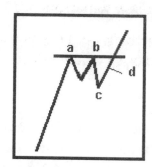

Reversal patterns of markets in strong uptrends attract eager top pickers. These patterns also shake out the nervous longs. When the reversal fails to follow through, these players are trapped on the wrong side of the market or knocked out.

The Double Top Knockout (DT-KO) seeks to take advantage of these traders' predicament as the shorts scramble to cover their positions and the longs that were shaken out are forced back in.

Here are the rules for the Double Top Knockout:

For Buys (Short Sales are reversed):

1. The market should be in a strong trend as defined by a computer-based indicator such as ADX >= 30 and +DMI > –DMI or as defined under Trend Qualifiers (Chapter 3).

2. The market must make a new two-month calendar high.

3. The market must make another new high no-sooner-than three trading days later. This is important as it allows the false double top to form.

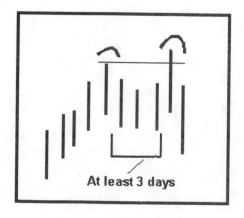

At least 3 days

4. The market must then make (at least) a two-bar low. This action draws in eager shorts (or shakes out longs) on what appears to be a confirmed double top. Buy tomorrow 1/16 above today's high.

5. If filled, place a protective stop 1/16 below yesterday's low. If this is more than 5% of the stock's value, risk no more than 5% of the stock's value.

Let's look at four examples.

FIGURE 6.5

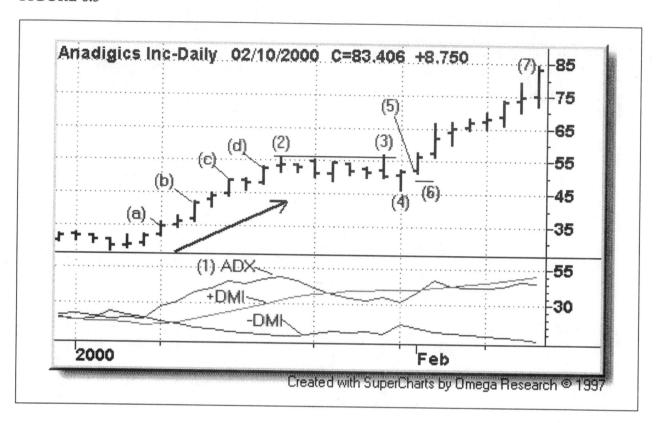

1. Anadigics (ANAD) qualifies as a strongly trending stock by having an ADX of 33 and +DMI > –DMI. Other Trend Qualifiers include its more than doubling in 10 days and having wide-range bars and strong closes in the direction of the trend (a), (b), (c) and (d).

2. The stock makes a new two-month high.

3. The stock makes another high six days later.

4. The stock sells off and trades below the two prior day's lows. Buy tomorrow at 52 1/16, 1/16 above today's high.

5. The stock trades at 52 1/16 and we go long.

6. The low of the setup is more than 5% away from our entry, so we place our protective stop at 49 7/16, 5% below our entry.

7. The trend resumes as the stock explodes more than 30 points over the next seven days.

FIGURE 6.6

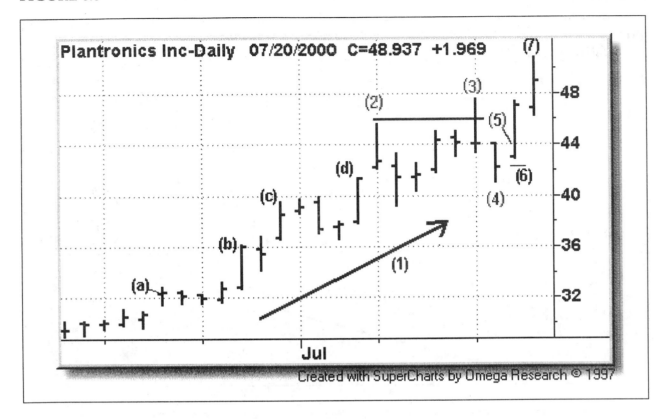

1. Plantronics (PLT) qualifies as being in a strong uptrend by having an ADX of 34 and +DMI > –DMI (not shown). Other Trend Qualifiers include its rallying nearly 70% in less than a month and a gap (a), its having wide-range bars (b), (c) and (d), and strong closes in the direction of the trend (b) and (d).

2. PLT makes a new two-month high.

3. The stock makes another new high five days later.

4. A two-bar low. Go long tomorrow 1/16 above today's high (44 1/16).

5. The stock trades at 44 1/16 and we go long.

6. Because the low of the setup is more than 5% away from our entry, we place a protective stop at 41 13/16 for a risk of 5%.

7. The stock trades over six points higher in two days.

Here's a low ADX example.

FIGURE 6.7

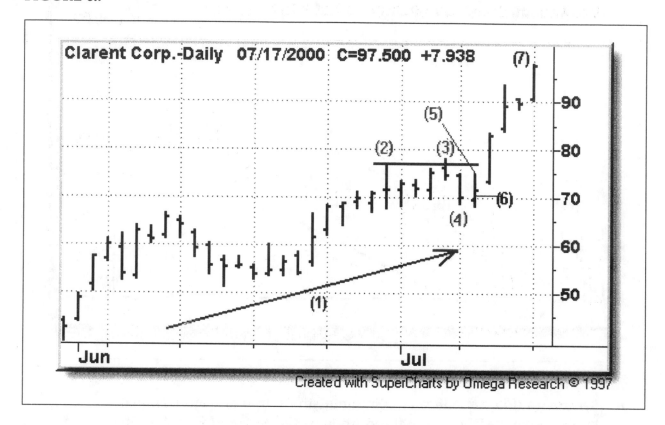

1. Clarent Corp. (CLRN) has a low ADX reading of 18 but qualifies as being in a strong trend by having rallied over 230% in less than a month.

2. The stock makes a new two-month high.

3. The stock makes another new high four days later.

4. The stock trades below the prior two lows. Go long tomorrow at 74 13/16, 1/16 above today's high.

5. The stock trades at 74 13/16 and we go long.

6. Because the low of the setup (68 7/16) is more than 5% away from our entry, we place our protective stop at 71 1/16 for a risk of 5%.

7. The trend resumes as the stocks rallies more than 22 points over the next four days.

FIGURE 6.8

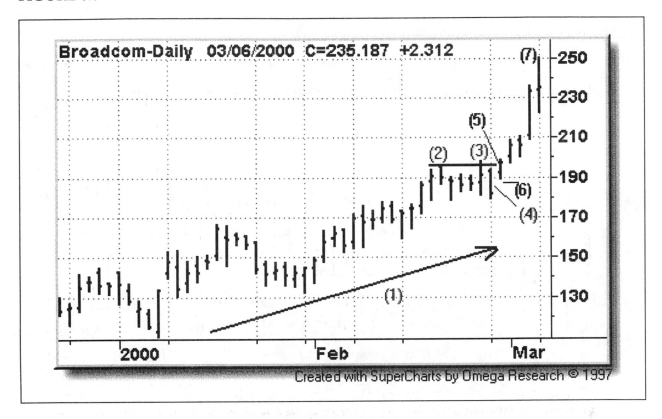

1. Broadcom (BRCM) has an ADX reading of 28 (not shown) but qualifies as being in a strong uptrend by its rising more than 80% in less than two months.

2. A two-month high.

3. Another two-month high four days later.

4. The stock trades below the two prior day's lows. Go long tomorrow at 193 3/8, 1/16 above today's high.

5. The stock trades at 193 3/8 and we go long.

6. Because the low of the setup (180) is more than 5% away from our entry, we place our protective stop at 183 11/16 for a risk of 5%.

7. The trend resumes as the stock explodes more than 50 points higher over the next five days.

Q&A

Q. How did you discover the DT-KO?

A. I know several very talented traders who are great at "putting their face in the fire" (going against the trend). When they are right, the payoff is substantial as they latch on to a major market turn. However, I noticed that more-often-than-not, they are quickly stopped out as the longer-term underlying trend resumes. I saw this fakeout as an opportunity.

Q. So you are basically taking the other side of their trades?

A. Yes and no. If the reversal is for real, my trade probably won't be triggered. However, if the reversal is false, then yes, I'm buying as the reversal players are getting stopped out.

Q. Why not play the double top and short the stock, then, look to reverse your position if stopped out (i.e. cover and go long)?

A. You could, but, again, I'd prefer going with the trend. Also, you would have to be very disciplined and willing to switch from bearish to bullish very quickly. Psychologically, this may be tough for many. Further, there are execution costs and risks in doing all those trades. You could probably make such a "stop and reverse" strategy work in futures where there isn't an uptick rule for shorting and the increased leverage would help to cover the execution costs.

TREND PIVOT (FALSE RALLY) PULLBACKS

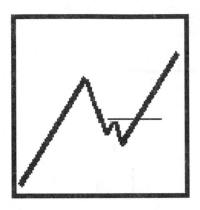

Like the Trend Knockout, here's another pattern born out of frustration. Often I would enter pullbacks and find myself quickly stopped out a few days before the market mounted a major move. This was difficult as I was "right" but too early. It's now obvious to me that the correction wasn't over and I should have been looking to re-enter the market as the trend resumed.

Trend Pivot Pullbacks seek to identify pullbacks that have had this false rally. This rally draws in, and subsequently shakes out the "fast money"—traders without staying power (money) and/or patience. Once these players are cleared out of the market, the stock often resumes its uptrend.

Here are the rules for the Trend Pivot Pullback:

For Buys (Short Sales are reversed):

1. The market should be in a strong trend as defined by a computer-based indicator such as ADX >= 30 and +DMI > –DMI or as defined under Trend Qualifiers (Chapter 3).

2. The market must make a two-month calendar high.

3. The market must subsequently make at least one, but no more than five, lower highs.

4. The market must stage a one-day rally (a high greater than the prior day's high) followed by a lower high. This is known as a pivot high and is illustrated below. Go long tomorrow or the next day 1/16 above this pivot high.

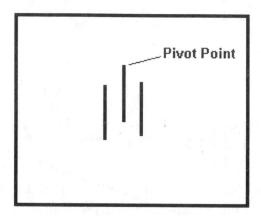

5. If filled, place a protective stop 1/16 below the lowest bar in the setup. If this is more than 5% of the stock's value, risk no more than 5% of the stock's value.

FIGURE 6.9

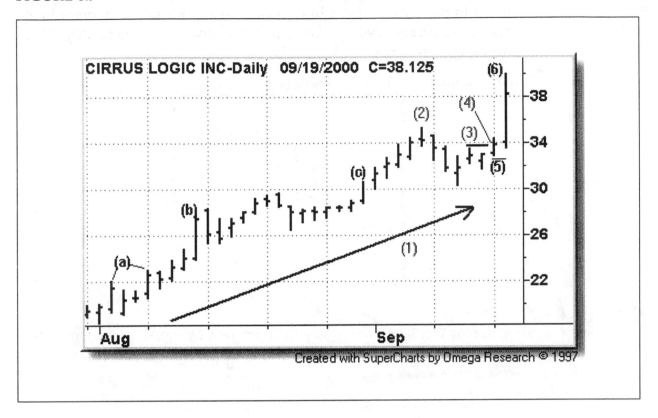

CIRRUS LOGIC INC-Daily   09/19/2000   C=38.125

Created with SuperCharts by Omega Research © 1997

1. Cirrus Logic (CRUS) qualifies as being in a strong uptrend by having an ADX of 49 and +DMI > –DMI (not shown). Other Trend Qualifiers include its nearly doubling in less than a month and having wide-range bars and strong closes (a) and (b) in the direction of the trend and a high-level base breakout (c).

2. The stock makes a new two-month high.

3. The stock begins rallying out of a pullback but fails, leaving a pivot point at 33 3/8. Go long tomorrow at 33 7/16, 1/16 above pivot high.

4. The stock trades at 33 7/16 and we go long.

5. Because the low of the setup (30 3/8) is more than 5% away from our entry, we place a protective stop at 31 3/4 for a risk of 5%.

6. The trend resumes and the stock rallies nearly 20% in two days.

Here's a low-ADX example.

FIGURE 6.10

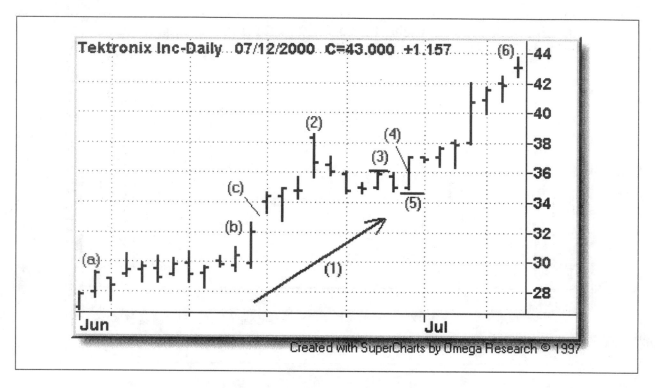

1. Tektronix (TEK) has a fairly low ADX of 25 (not shown) but qualifies as being in a strong trend by rising nearly 60% in less than a month. Other Trend Qualifiers include its having wide-range bars (a) and (b), a gap (c), and strong closes in the direction of the uptrend (a) and (b).

2. Tektronix makes a new two-month calendar high.

3. After three lower highs, the stock begins rallying out of a pullback but fails on 6/29/2000 leaving a pivot point at 35 15/16 (the high of the previous day). Go long 1/16 above the pivot high (36) tomorrow or the next day.

4. The stock trades at 36 and we go long.

5. Place a protective stop at 34 5/8, 1/16 below the low of the formation.

6. The trend resumes as the stock trades more than 20% higher over the next eight days.

Here's another low-ADX example.

FIGURE 6.11

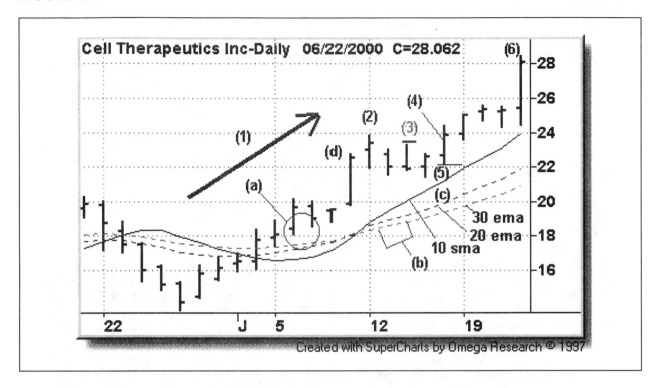

1. Cell Therapeutics has a low ADX (17) but is in a strong uptrend based on the fact that it has risen over 70% in just over two weeks. Other Trend Qualifiers include its having Daylight (a), positive slopes on the 10-period simple, 20-period exponential and 30-period exponential moving averages (b), proper order (10SMA>20EMA>30EMA) of its moving average (c) and its having a wide-range bar higher with a strong close (d).

2. The stock makes a new two-month high.

3. The stock has a one-day false rally, forming a pivot point at 23 1/4 (a lower high the day before and lower high the day after). Go long tomorrow or the next day at 23 5/16, 1/16 above the pivot high.

4. The stock trades at 23 5/16 and we go long.

5. Because the low of the setup (21 1/2) is more than 5% away from our entry, we place a protective stop at 22 1/8 for a risk of 5%.

6. The trend resumes as the stock trades more than 20% higher over the next five days.

Here's a low-ADX example on the short side.

FIGURE 6.12

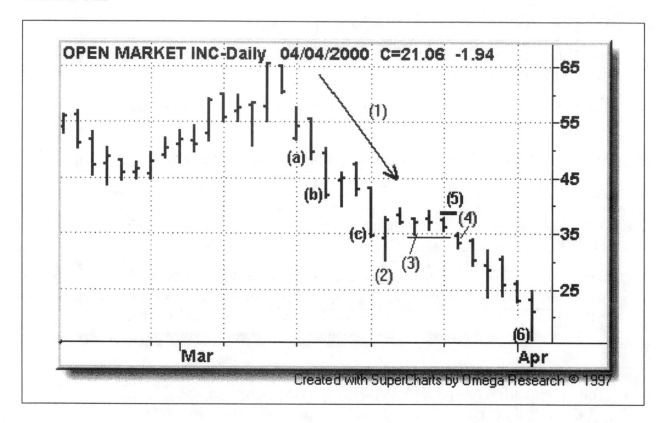

1. Open Market (OMKT) has a low ADX of 22 but is in an obvious downtrend by losing over half of its value in seven days. Other Trend Qualifiers include its having wide-range bars lower and poor closes (a), (b) and (c).

2. The stock makes a new two-month low.

3. The stock forms a pivot point (a low surrounded by two *higher* lows). Go short tomorrow or the next day at 35 1/16, 1/16 below the pivot low.

4. The stock opens at 34 ½ and we go short.

5. Because the high of the setup is more than 5% away from our entry, we place a protective stop at 36 1/4 for a risk of 5%

6. The downtrend resumes as the stock implodes, losing over 50% of its value over the next six days.

Q&A

Q. Should the pivot high be less than the two-month high (rule 1)?

A. Yes, otherwise it wouldn't be a pullback

Q. Don't you give up some of the move by requiring the stock to trade back above the pivot high?

A. Yes, but you also often avoid getting caught in a potential second false move.

Q. So when it trades above the pivot high, it helps confirm the rally?

A. Yes.

Q. What's the difference between this pattern and the Simple Pullback (SP)?

A. The SP doesn't require the one-day false rally. With the Simple pullbacks, you actually enter the market on that false rally. Of course, at that time, you don't know that it's going to turn out to be a false rally.

Q. So why not wait until a Trend Pivot Pullback is formed?

A. You could. It all depends on your trading style. However, you will miss all of the stocks that don't come back in. For me, its tough to watch all these stocks go by.

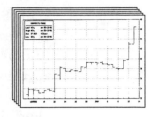

CHAPTER 7

BOW TIES

▪ ▫ ▪ ▫ ▪ ▫ ▪ ▫ ▪ ▫ ▪ ▫ ▪ ▫ ▪ ▫ ▪ ▫ ▪ ▫ ▪ ▫ ▪ ▫ ▫ ▪ ▫

Picking tops and bottoms can be costly, as markets are prone to long-term continuation moves and false reversals. On the other hand, blindly jumping on an established trend can also be costly, as these markets are prone to correct. Bow Ties avoid these pitfalls associated with trend trading and top/bottom picking by waiting for the trend to turn based on multiple moving averages followed by a countertrend correction.

In Chapter 3, Trend Qualifiers, we defined "proper order" for an uptrend as when the faster moving averages (shorter periods) were above the slower moving averages (longer periods). Conversely, for a downtrend, we defined proper order as when the faster moving averages were below the slower moving averages.

With Bow Ties, we are looking for these moving averages to switch from downtrend proper order to uptrend proper order over a period of three to four days. This gives the moving averages the appearance of a bow tie as they all cross and spread out from one point. When the Bow Tie forms, it suggests that the market has made a major trend shift. However, it's still prone to correct. Therefore, Bow Ties seek to enter *after* a minor correction.

Here are the rules for Bow Ties.

For Buys (Short Sales are reversed):

Using a 10-period simple, 20-period exponential and a 30-period exponential moving average:

1. The moving averages should converge and spread out again, shifting from proper downtrend order (10-SMA < 20-EMA < 30-EMA) to proper uptrend order (10-SMA > 20-EMA >30-EMA). Ideally, this should happen over a period of three to four days. This creates the appearance of a bow tie in the averages. This is illustrated below.

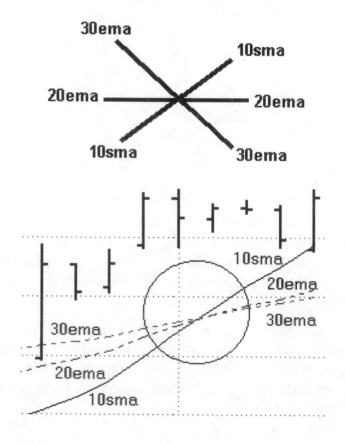

2. The market must make a lower low. That is, today's low must be less than yesterday's low.

3. Once qualifications for (2) have been met. Place a buy order 1/16 above today's high good for tomorrow. Continue to work an order above today's high good for the next trading day until filled or the market trades below its 20-period exponential moving average.

4. If filled, place a protective stop below the lowest bar in the setup. If this is extreme, then place your stop no more than 5% away from your entry.

Let's look at five examples.

FIGURE 7.1

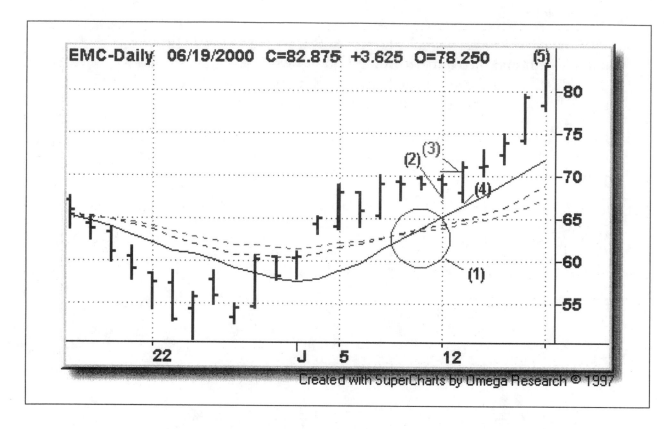

1. The moving averages on EMC converge and begin to spread out.

2. A lower low. Go long at 69 15/16, 1/16 above today's high.

3. The stock trades at 69 15/16 and we go long.

4. Place a protective stop at 67 1/16, 1/16 below the low of the setup.

5. The trend resumes as the stock rallies nearly 13 points over the next four days.

FIGURE 7.2

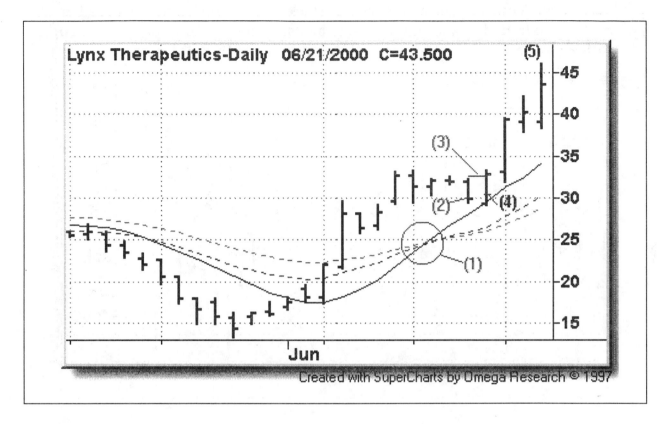

1. The moving averages converge on Lynx Therapeutics (LYNX) and begin to spread out—giving the appearance of a "bow tie."

2. A lower low. Go long tomorrow at 32 3/16, 1/16 above today's high.

3. The stock trades at 32 3/16 and we go long.

4. Because the low of the setup (29 1/4) is more than 5% away from our entry, we place our protective stop at 30 9/16 for a risk of 5%.

5. The uptrend continues as the stock trades 40% higher over the next four days.

Here's an example on the short side in the Nasdaq Composite. Signals in indices can help you time your stock market entries and exits or they can be traded in and of themselves by using index futures or holder shares.

FIGURE 7.3

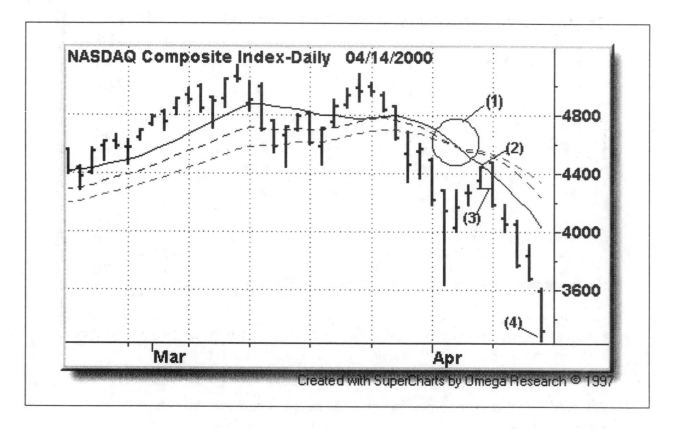

1. The moving averages on the Nasdaq Composite converge and begin to spread out as the index rolls over.

2. The index makes a higher high. Go short tomorrow if the index trades below today's low (4323).

3. The index trades below the low of (2), 4322, triggering a signal.

4. The index loses over 1,000 points, nearly 25%, over the next four days.

Here's an example in the futures market.

FIGURE 7.4

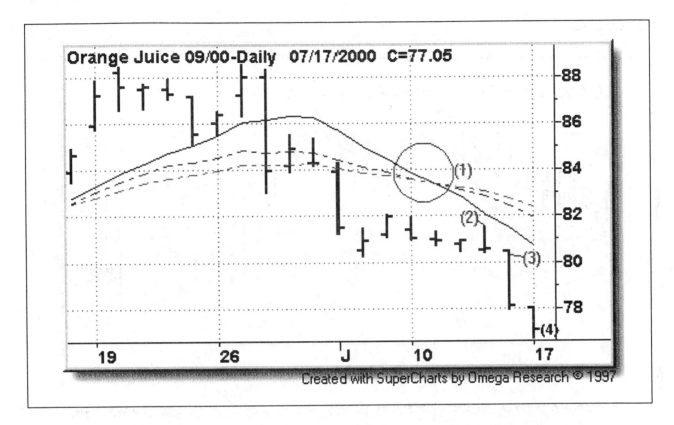

1. On 7/12/2000, the moving averages on September Orange Juice converge and begin to spread out as the market rolls over from an uptrend to a downtrend.

2. The market trades above the prior-day high.

3. A signal is triggered as the market trades below the low of (2).

4. OJ drops over 3 points in two days.

Here's an example of no fill.

FIGURE 7.5

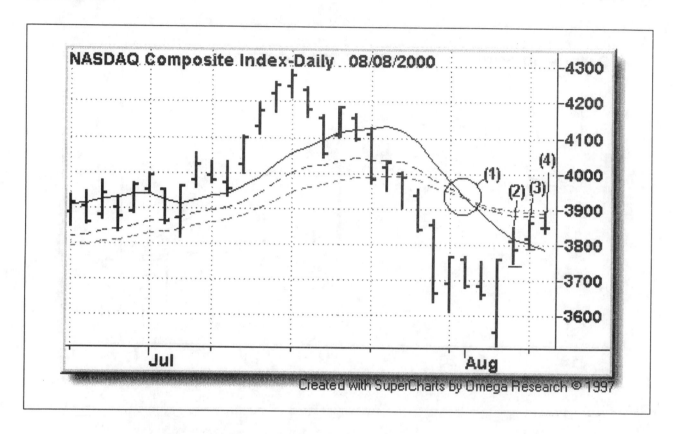

1. The moving averages on the Nasdaq Composite converge and begin to spread out again.

2. A higher high. Go short tomorrow 1-point below today's low.

3. No fill and another higher high. Go short tomorrow 1 point below today's low.

4. The index trades above its 20-day exponential moving average. Cancel order.

Q&A

Q.   Why use multiple moving averages?

A.   When several moving averages converge at the middle of the Bow Tie, it suggests that the longer term and shorter cycles are coming together. Once they spread out again, it suggests a new trend is being formed.

Q.   So why not just buy the market as soon as it comes out of the convergence?

A.   In spite of what many books on technical analysis will tell you, moving-average crossovers *do not* work. I suppose in their defense, many of these books were written before everyone had a computer sitting on their desk. Before computers, crossovers worked much better.

Q.   Do you think they used to work better because it wasn't so obvious?

A.   Yes. Technology has helped to eradicate this edge.

Q.   Back to Bow Ties, does the countertrend movement (rule #2, a lower low for buys and a higher high for short sales) help to eliminate false starts?

A.   Exactly. You often avoid false moves by waiting for a countertrend by only entering if the trend re-asserts itself. Conceptually, it's no different than pullbacks. Essentially, you are looking for thrust/trend, correction and then resumption of trend.

Q.   Why cancel your entry order if the market trades back to the 20-day EMA?

A.   If a market comes all the way back to the 20-day EMA, it's possible that what appeared to be a new trend is a false move. This doesn't mean that the market isn't worthy of trading. As you know, in trading there are no exacts. However, in any pattern, you should have a rule for when you should step back and re-evaluate your analysis. Maybe some other pattern is forming? Maybe not.

Q.   But it's okay for the market to trade back to the 10-day simple moving average?

A.   I think it's normal, and likely healthy, for a market to pull back to the 10-day SMA.

Q. You refer to the Bow Tie from downtrend to uptrend for longs and uptrend to downtrend for shorts. Does the pattern work on markets coming out of consolidations or bases?

A. Yes. I discovered the pattern while studying markets that had major changes in trend—from up to down or from down to up. The beauty is that you avoid top and bottom picking by waiting for a confirmation of this rollover. A "half bow tie," if you will, emerges when the price is coming out of bases/consolidations. These seem to work, but I prefer the "rollover" pattern, as the chance exists that there are players still trapped on the wrong side of the market.

Q. The "trapped" players will add fuel to the rally or sell-off for short set-ups?

A. Yes.

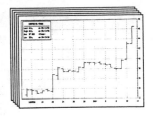

CHAPTER **8**

MICRO PATTERNS

HIGH-LEVEL MICRO DOUBLE BOTTOM

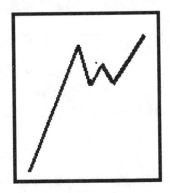

As its name implies, a double bottom is normally considered a bottoming pattern as a market in a downtrend bottoms, has a false rally and then makes a final bottom at or slightly above the previous bottom. However, sometimes a market is so strong that it's able to make the formation as part of a continuation move. In other words, it sells off very little while forming this pattern. This is known as a high-level double bottom and is shown in Figure 8.1.

FIGURE 8.1

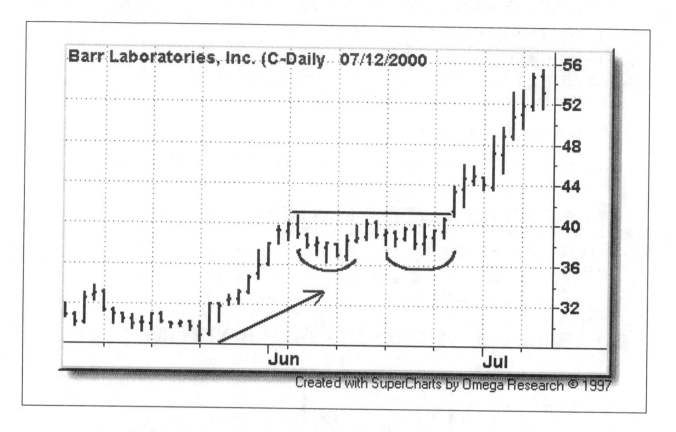

Corrections such as the above normally take place over several weeks to months. Sometimes, however, stocks are so strong that they will correct over much shorter time frames—forming a "micro" pattern.

Although still a discretionary pattern in nature, the High-Level Micro Double Bottom is more easily defined than its bigger picture counterpart. We define the pattern as two pivot lows which form at or near the same level. To review, a pivot low is formed when a stock makes a lower low followed by a higher low. This leaves a low surrounded by two higher lows.

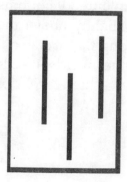

Here are the rules for the High-Level Micro Double Bottom

For Buys (Short sales are reversed):

1. The market should be in a strong trend as defined by a computer-based indicator such as ADX >= 30 and +DMI > –DMI or as defined under Trend Qualifiers (Chapter 3).

2. The stock must make at least a two-month.

3. The stock must make a pivot low, that is, a low surrounded by two higher lows.

4. The stock must make another pivot low at or near the first pivot low.

5. Go long 1/16 above the high of the right side of the pivot low formed in (4).

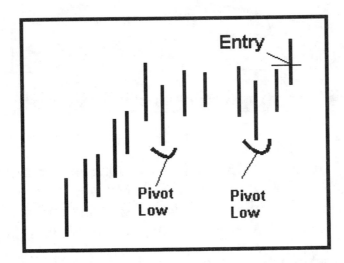

6. If filled, place a protective stop below the lowest bar in the setup. If this is more than 5% of the stock's value, risk no more than 5%.

FIGURE 8.2

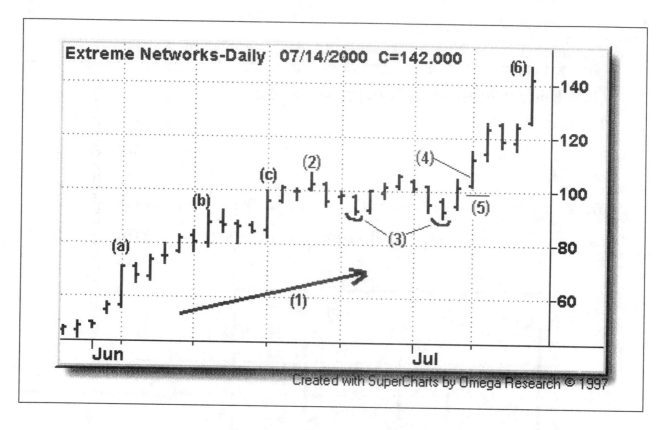

1. Extreme Networks (EXTR) qualifies as being in a strong uptrend by having an ADX of 37 and +DMI > –DMI (not shown). Other Trend Qualifiers include its more than doubling in less than a month and its having wide-range bars higher (a), (b) and strong closes (a), (c).

2. The stock makes a new two-month high.

3. The stock forms two pivot lows near the same price level. Go long tomorrow at 104 3/4, 1/16 above the high of the second pivot formation.

4. The stock trades at 104 3/4 and we go long.

5. Because the low of the setup (90 5/8), is more than 5% away from our entry, we place our protective stop at 99 ½ for a risk of 5%.

6. The uptrend resumes as the stock trades more than 40% higher over the next five days.

Here we have two back-to-back examples in Sonus Networks, a hot IPO.

FIGURE 8.3

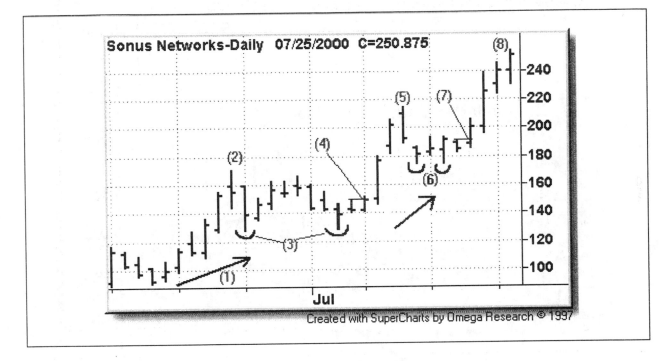

1. Sonus Networks (SONS) qualifies as being in a strong uptrend by rising over 80% since its offering. (Note: ADX is not applicable on new issues.)

2. The stock makes a new high.

3. The stock forms two pivot points six days apart near the same price level.

4. The stock trades above the high of the second pivot formation and we go long at 148 1/16, 1/16 above the pivot formation.

5. The stock trades over 57 points higher in three days and makes a new high.

6. The stock forms two pivot lows one day apart near the same price level.

7. The stock trades above the high of the second pivot formation and we go long at 191 1/16, 1/16 above the pivot formation.

8. The stock trades 40 points higher over the next four days.

Here we have an example in the Amex Biotech Index (BTK). Sector signals can be used to help time entries in individual stocks within that sector or can be traded in and of themselves through holder shares or sector options.

FIGURE 8.4

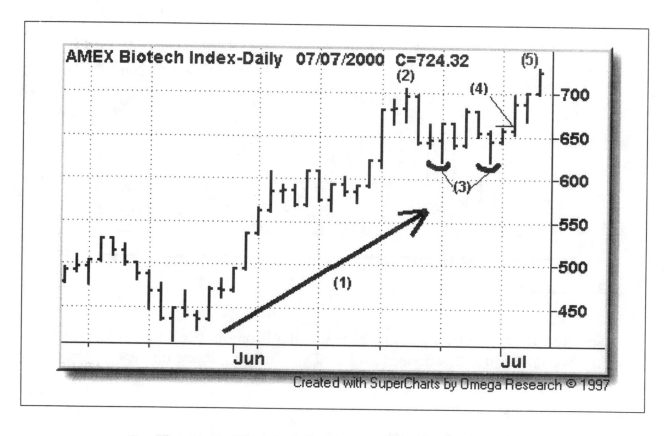

1. The Amex Biotech Index has an ADX below 30 (29) (not shown), but qualifies as being in a strong uptrend by its rising over 70% in less than a month. Other Trend Qualifiers include it having wide-range bars higher and strong closes.

2. The index makes a new two-month high.

3. The index forms two pivot lows three days apart near the same price level.

4. The index trades above the high of the second pivot formation, signaling an entry.

5. The trend resumes as the index rises over 100 points in three days.

Q&A

Q.   How did you begin noticing High-Level Micro Double Bottoms?

A.   Pullbacks are my favorite patterns. Many times I'd notice that even though a stock didn't follow though on a rally out of a pullback, it still didn't do anything wrong.

Q.   Define wrong.

A.   It would come back and test the level of the original pullback. I noticed that this became a level of strong support.

HIGH-LEVEL MICRO CUP AND HANDLE

The cup-and-handle pattern, popularized by William O'Neil, often precedes large market moves. The pattern forms when a market sells off, bases (consolidates), rallies back up to the area of its original sell-off, and finally, pulls back to form the handle. Cup and handles are traded in the same fashion as pullbacks.

FIGURE 8.5

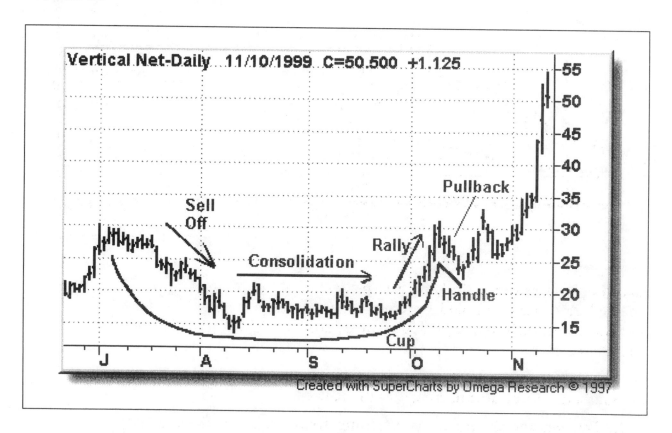

Sometimes a market is so strong that it will form a bottoming pattern within a trend. This is known as a running correction. Therefore, I have dubbed cup and handles that form during strong trends and above their 50-day moving averages as "Running Cup and Handles" (originally published in *The Trading Markets Guide to Conquering The Markets*). This combines the best of both worlds: momentum and a bottoming pattern. An example of a Running Cup and Handle is shown in Figure 8.6.

FIGURE 8.6

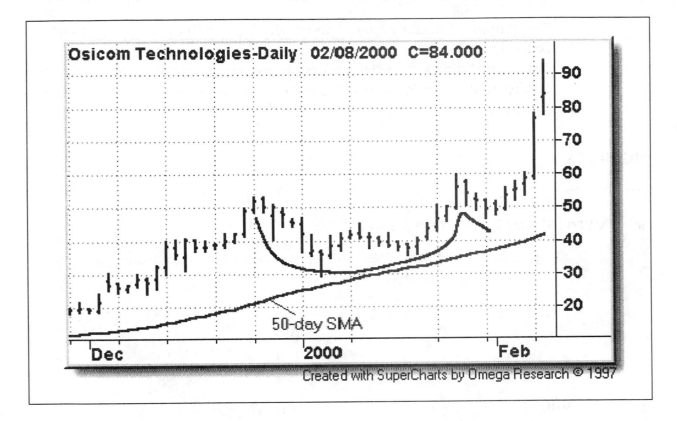

Taken one step further, stocks in extremely strong trends often form compressed or "micro" cup and handles. These occur over a period of days as opposed to their bigger picture counterparts, which may take weeks to months to form.

Although discretionary in nature, the following rules and examples should help you be able to recognize the pattern.

1. The market should be in a strong trend as defined by a computer-based indicator such as ADX >= 30 and +DMI > –DMI or as defined under Trend Qualifiers (Chapter 3).

2. The market must make a two-month high.

3. The market should have a one to four day sell-off (a). This action forms the left side of the cup.

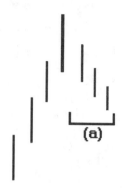

4. The market must then trade sideways for one to four days (b). This action forms the bottom of the cup.

5. The market must then rally back up to at or near the original sell-off (c). This action forms the right side of the cup.

6. The market should pull back for two to four days. Ideally, this should be no more than 50% to 60% of the depth of the cup (d). This action forms the handle.

7. Once the above rules have been met. Go long tomorrow, 1/16 above today's high.

8. If filled, place an initial protective stop (IPS) below the low of the handle. If this is more than 5% of the stock's value, risk no more than 5%.

FIGURE 8.7

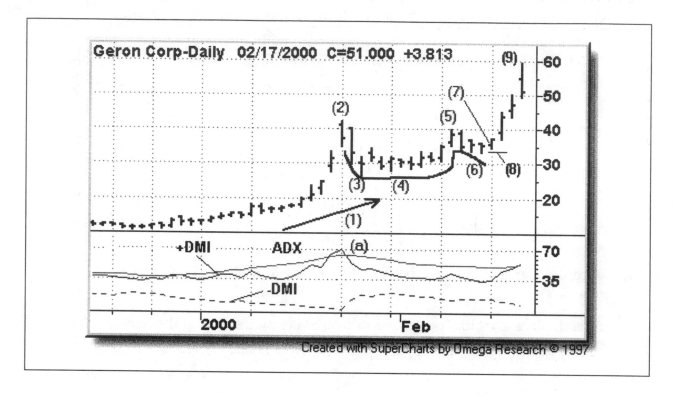

1. Geron (GERN) qualifies as being in a strong trend by having an ADX reading of 64 and +DMI > –DMI (a) and by having risen over 400% in a month.

2. The stock makes a new two-month high.

3. The stock begins to sell-off, forming the left side of the cup.

4. The stock trades sideways, forming the bottom of the cup.

5. The stock rallies to near the level of the original sell-off, forming the right side of the cup.

6. The stock drifts lower. The action forms the handle and completes the cup. Go long tomorrow at 36 1/16, 1/16 above today's high.

7. The stock trades at 36 1/16 and we go long.

8. Because the low of the handle (33 3/4) is more than 5% away from our entry, we place our protective stop at 34 1/4 for a risk of 5%. Note: In cases like this when the pattern-based protective stop is slightly greater than 5%, you could use the pattern-based stop (in this case, the low of the handle) and trade fewer shares to compensate for the added risk.

9. The trend resumes as the stock nearly doubles over the next four days.

FIGURE 8.8

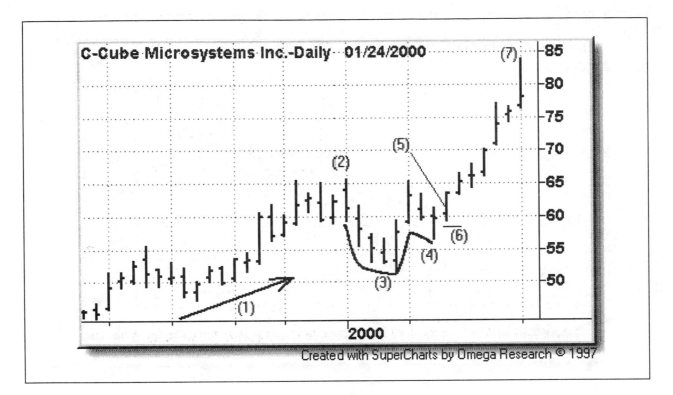

1. C-Cube Microsystems (CUBE) qualifies as being in a strong uptrend by having an ADX of 46 and +DMI > –DMI (not shown) and by having risen more than 40% in less than three weeks.

2. The stock makes a two-month high.

3. The stock sells off, trades sideways and rallies to near the level of the sell-off. This action forms the cup.

4. The stock sells off, forming the handle. Go long tomorrow at 61 5/16, 1/16 above today's high.

5. The stock trades at 61 5/16 and we go long.

6. Because the low of the setup (56 3/4) is more than 5% away from our entry, we place our protective stop at 58 1/4 for a risk of 5%.

7. The trend resumes as the stock explodes more than 40% higher over the next seven days.

FIGURE 8.9

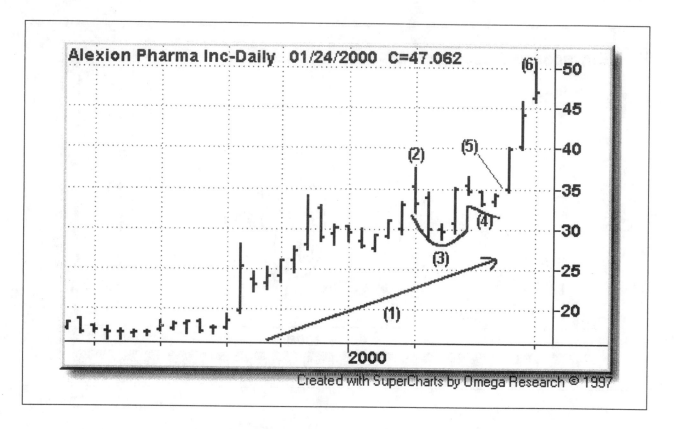

1. Alexion Pharmaceuticals is in a strong uptrend.

2. The stock makes a new two-month high.

3. The stock sells off and then trades sideways and rallies back up near the level of the two-month high (2). This action forms the cup.

4. The stock then drifts lower to form the handle. Go long tomorrow at 34 11/16, 1/16 above today's high.

5. The stock gaps open to 35 and we go long.

6. The stock explodes over 40% higher as the trend continues.

FIGURE 8.10

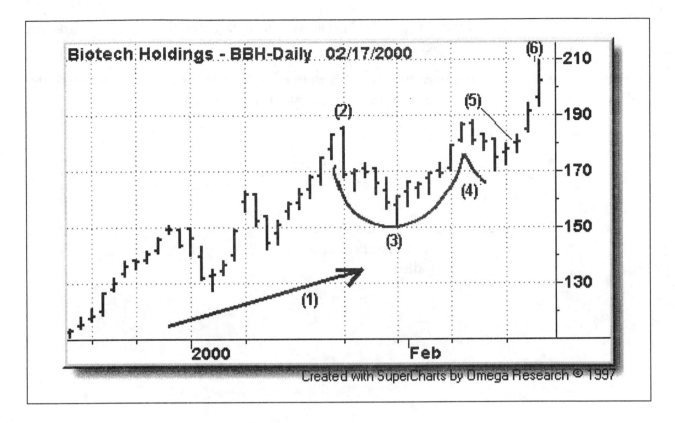

1. The Biotech HOLDRS (BBH) are in a strong uptrend.

2. The shares make a new two-month high.

3. The shares sell off, trade sideways and then rally back up near the level of the original sell-off. This action forms the cup.

4. The shares drift lower forming a handle. Go long tomorrow at 179 7/16, 1/16 above today's high.

5. The shares trade at 179 7/16 and we go long.

6. The trend resumes as the shares rally over 28 points in three days.

Q&A

Q.   The Micro Cup and Handle seems very discretionary. Any tips on how to recognize them?

A.   The best way to learn this pattern is to look at charts, lots of charts. After a while, you'll find your eye drawn to the pattern.

Q.   Any other tips?

A.   Yes, look for other patterns that may also be setting up.

Q.   Such as?

A.   Double Top Knockouts that don't trigger immediately often set up as Micro Cup and Handles. Also, sometimes pullbacks set up as Micro Cup and Handles.

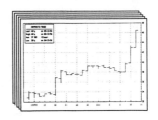

SECTION THREE

VOLATILITY

. . . .

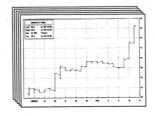

CHAPTER **9**

FINDING EXPLOSIVE MOVES: AN ADVANCED LESSON IN SWING TRADING

□ □

> *We predict that the use of historical volatility will be*
> *one of the growth areas for financial markets in the*
> *late '90s. Up until now, the use of historical volatility*
> *has been confined mostly to the options market, but*
> *we have found it can be equally applied to the*
> *futures and equity markets.*
>
> — Connors and Hayward,
> *Investment Secrets of a*
> *Hedge Fund Manager*

As swing traders, our goal is to find markets that have the potential to make large moves over a short time frame. One of the greatest tools that can help us accomplish this goal is the study of volatility. Although the concepts can be a little overwhelming at first, I can assure you that they are well worth your effort to learn them.

HISTORICAL VOLATILITY

Historical volatility (HV), also known as statistical volatility, is the standard deviation of day-to-day price changes expressed as an annual percentage. Its complete calculation can be found in the appendix. However, don't get too caught up in the details of the formula and have your computer do the work for you. Just know that it's a measurement of how much a stock has fluctuated in the past and can be used as a gauge for how much the stock will *likely* fluctuate going forward. For instance, suppose the 50-day HV on a $100 stock is 10%. Assuming a normal distribution of stock prices and that volatility remains the same, this stock has a 66% chance (one standard deviation) of trading between $90 ($100 less 10%) and $110 ($100 + 10%) one year from now.

Again, don't get too caught up in the math. The main thing you should know about HV is that stocks with higher HV readings have fluctuated more in the past than stocks with lower HV readings. And further, those stocks with higher HV readings will likely fluctuate more in the future than those stocks with lower HV stocks. Therefore, as a short-term trader, we must focus on those stocks with higher HV readings as we are looking for an immediate move.

TRADING WHERE THE ACTION IS

Larry Connors, a pioneer in volatility research for the stock and commodity markets, has dubbed using HV to select stocks "Trading Where The Action Is." In *Connors On Advanced Trading,* he states: "As short-term traders, we do not have the luxury of waiting for a market to move. Because our profits tend to be small, we need to be trading those specific markets that provide us with the opportunity to maximize our profits on a daily basis."

I fully agree with Larry. As an example of the potential for higher HV stocks, refer to Figure 9.1 of Geron Corp. The stock had a 50-day HV reading of 95% in late 1999. This suggested that the stock statistically had the potential (a 66% chance) to trade either 95% higher or 95% lower over the next year. Notice that the stock skyrockets over the next few months and trades nearly 700% higher. It then tops out and loses 80% of its value in the following months. As you can see, stocks with higher HV readings have the potential to make extraordinary moves. In fact, all of the examples used in this manual had a 50-day HV reading of at least 40% and most had readings of 80% or higher.

FIGURE 9.1

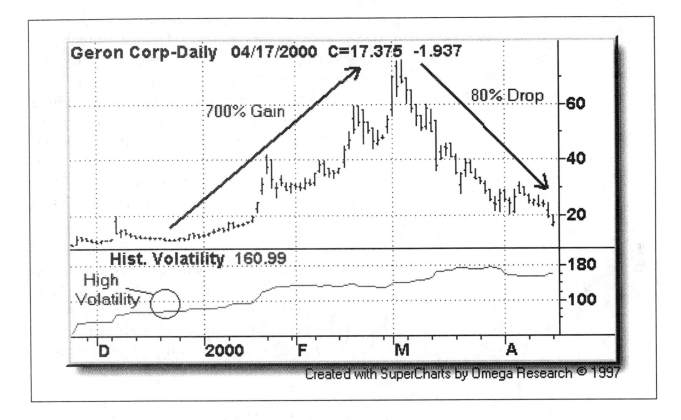

APPLYING HV

I use HV a lot like I use ADX. I don't plot it on each and every chart. Rather, I use it as a filtering tool when (computer) scanning through stocks. That is, by requiring the stocks have an HV reading of 40% or higher, it helps to weed out stocks with less potential.

MEAN REVERSION

In *Option Volatility and Pricing Strategies*, Sheldon Natenberg states that volatility tends to be mean (average) reverting. This complex concept can best be described in a joke: If you know someone who's normally mean and they are nice to you for a few days, chances are they will revert back to being mean. Seriously, "mean reversion" suggests that lower-than-normal volatility levels will revert back to higher or more average readings.

In *Investment Secrets Of A Hedge Fund Manager*, Larry Connors and Blake Hayward expanded on Natenberg's work and showed that when shorter term HV readings dropped below 50% of their longer-term HV readings, a large market move was prone to ensue as volatility reverts back to its mean.

As an example, referring to Figure 9.2, Analog Devices (ADI), notice that the six-day HV reading (33.39) dropped to less than half of the 100-day HV Reading (68.39) as the stock traded sideways. Referring to Figure 9.3, the stock explodes higher (a) as the short-term volatility reverts back to more normal longer-term levels (b).

FIGURE 9.2

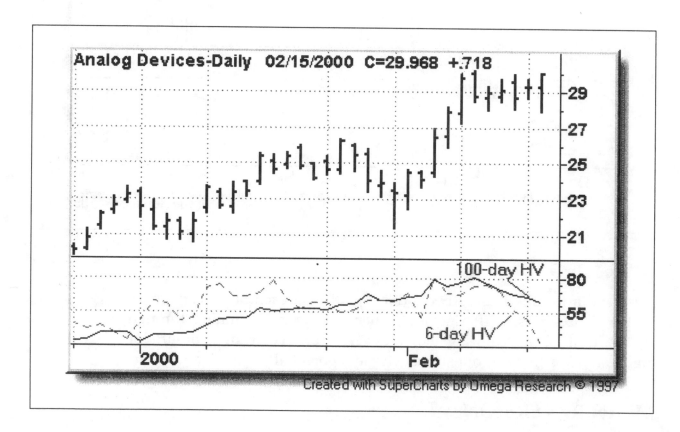

FIGURE 9.3

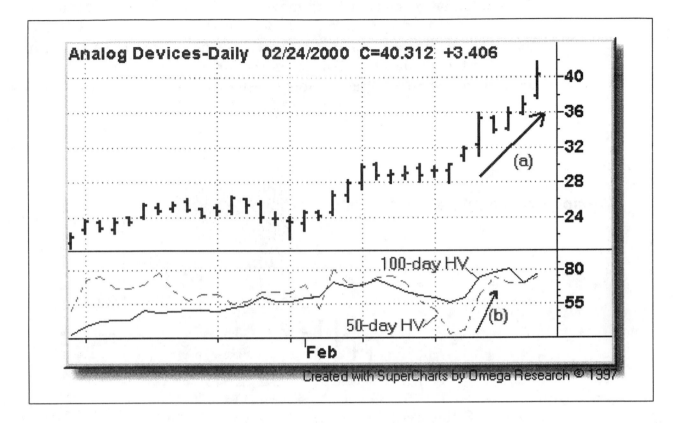

Although Connors and Hayward showed that large moves often occur out of low-volatility situations, they did not attempt to predict the direction of the move. They stated: *"The Connors-Hayward Historical Volatility System has an uncanny ability to predict major moves. Unfortunately, it does not tell you in which direction the move will be. Therefore, the strategy you select will depend upon the strategies and indicators you are comfortable with."*

I agree with Connors and Hayward. Therefore, when I encounter a market that has low short-term volatility readings versus its longer-term, I look for setups described in this manual that might suggest which way the market is headed.

HV RATIOS

Before we get into examples of applying short- versus long-term volatility readings to stocks, let's look at an easier way to recognize this relationship. This relationship can be expressed as a ratio. That is, to divide the shorter-term HV (six-day) reading by the longer-term (100-day) volatility reading. When the ratio drops below 50%, we know that the market has the potential to make a large move as volatility reverts back to its mean. Figure 9.4, is the same stock described earlier except that the 100-day HV reading and six-day HV readings have been replaced with the ratio of the six-day HV divided by the 100-day HV. Notice that the ratio drops below 50% (a) right before the stock makes a large move (b).

FIGURE 9.4

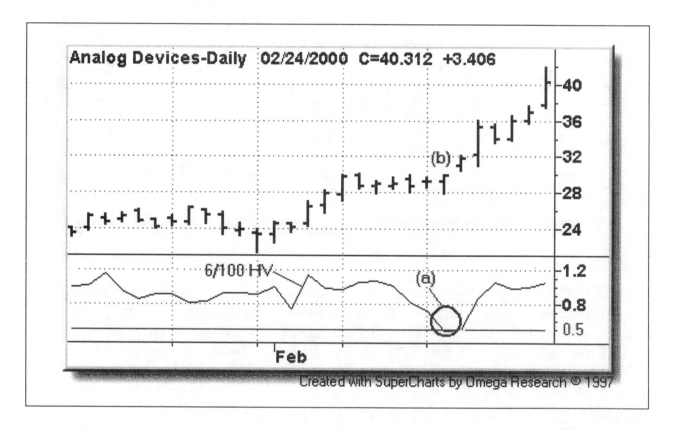

Let's look at some swing-trade setups that also had low 6/100 HV-ratio readings.

Here we have an example of a Trend Pivot Pullback with a low 6/100 HV ratio.

FIGURE 9.5

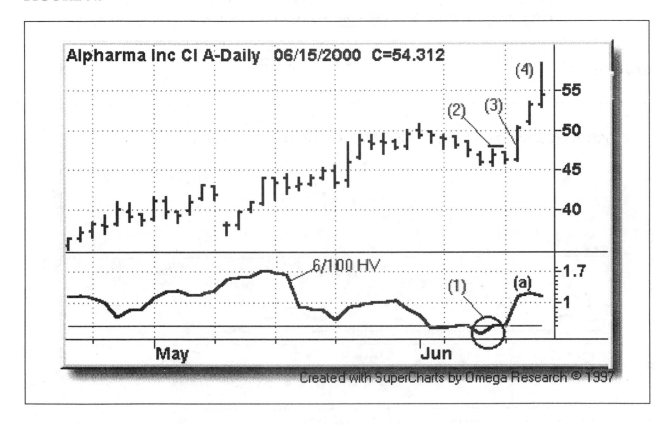

1. Alpharma (ALO) has 6-day HV/100-day HV reading below 50%. This suggests a large move is imminent, as volatility is prone to revert back to its mean.

2. The stock sets up as a Trend Pivot Pullback (see Chapter 6 for details).

3. An entry is triggered on the Trend Pivot Pullback.

4. The stock explodes higher as volatility reverts back to its mean (a).

Here we have an example of a High-Level Micro Double Bottom with low 6/100 HV readings.

FIGURE 9.6

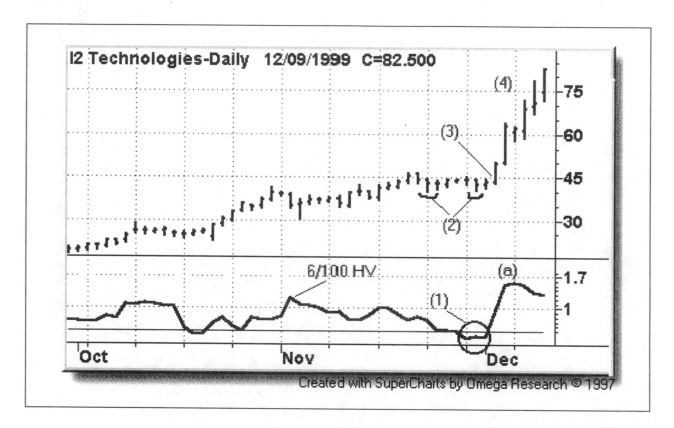

1. I2 Technologies (ITWO) has 6-day HV/100-day HV reading below 50%. This suggests a large move is imminent, as volatility is prone to revert back to its mean.

2. The stock sets up as a High-Level Micro Double Bottom (see Chapter 8 for details).

3. An entry is triggered on the High-Level Micro Double Bottom.

4. The stock explodes higher as volatility reverts back to its mean (a).

FIGURE 9.7

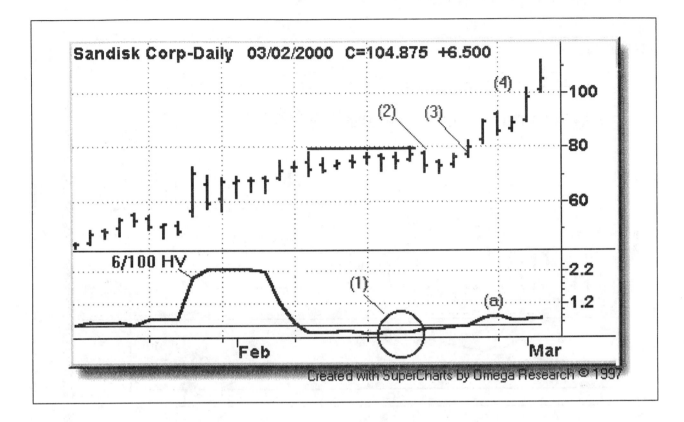

1. Sandisk (SNDK) has a 6-day HV/100-day HV reading below 50%. This suggests a large move is imminent, as volatility is prone to revert back to its mean.

2. The stock sets up as a Double Top Knockout (see Chapter 6 for details).

3. This is where discretion comes in. Although the Double Top Knockout didn't trigger right after the setup (day one), the fact that the stock held at high levels and began to rally, combined with a low-volatility situation, made the setup still worthy of considering. Therefore, when the stock trades above the entry of the DT-KO, we go long.

4. The stock explodes over 30 points higher as volatility reverts back to its mean.

Here we have an example of a shallow pullback with low 6/100 HV readings.

FIGURE 9.8

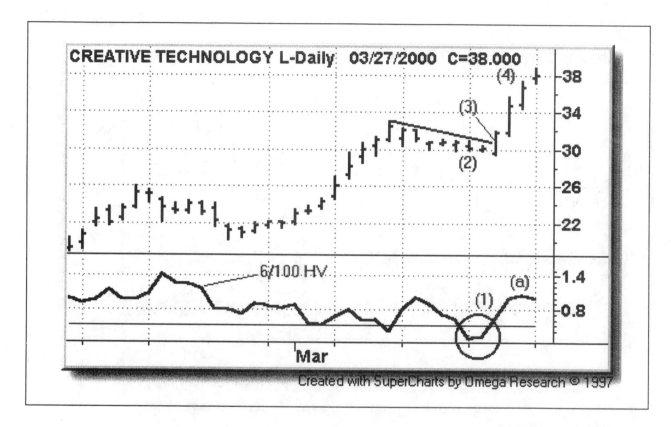

1. Creative Technology (CREAF) has a 6-day HV/100-day HV reading below 50%. This suggests a large move is imminent, as volatility is prone to revert back to its mean.

2. The stock, which has been in a strong uptrend, forms a seven-bar shallow pullback.

3. An entry is triggered on the pullback.

4. The stock explodes higher as volatility reverts back to its mean (a).

Here's another example of a shallow pullback with low 6/100 HV readings.

FIGURE 9.9

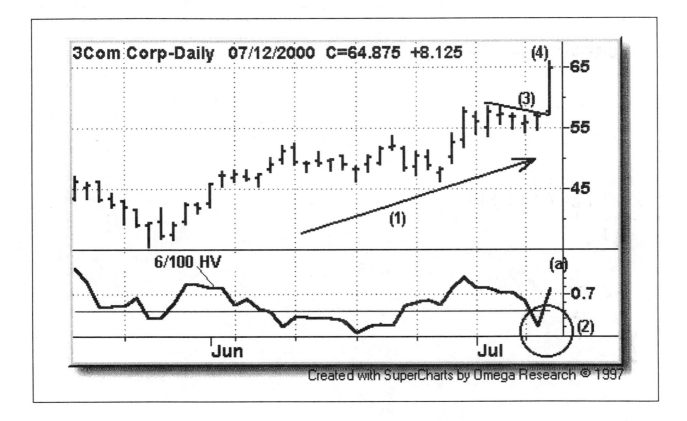

1. 3Com (COMS) is in a strong uptrend.

2. The 6/100 HV ratio drops below 50%. This suggests a large move is imminent as volatility is prone to revert back to its mean.

3. At the same time, the stock sets up as a shallow pullback.

4. The stock explodes nearly 20% higher in one day, as volatility reverts to its mean (a).

SECTION FOUR

MARKET TIMING

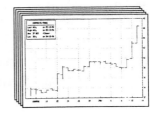

CHAPTER **10**

MARKET TIMING FOR SWING TRADING

◘ ◘

A rising tide lifts all boats.

— old Wall Street adage

In this chapter, we will look at how to gauge the overall direction of the market to help time swing trades. This involves discretionary analysis, system analysis and sector analysis.

DISCRETIONARY ANALYSIS

When analyzing the overall indices, I first look for any Trend Qualifiers that might suggest an overall trend. These include how the market is trading relative to its 10-SMA, 20-EMA and 30-EMAs (Daylight, slope, proper order). I also look for setups and concepts described in this manual, such as Trend Knockouts (TKOs), Simple Pullbacks (SP), etc. I check for these on both the cash indices and in the futures market. As an example (Figure 10.1), notice that in the sharp uptrend of the Nasdaq Composite from November of 1999 through January of 2000 there were Trend Qualifiers in the moving averages such as positive slope and Daylight, and they were in proper uptrend order. Also notice that there were setups such as Trend Knockouts (TKOs) and Simple Pullbacks (SP) along the way.

FIGURE 10.1

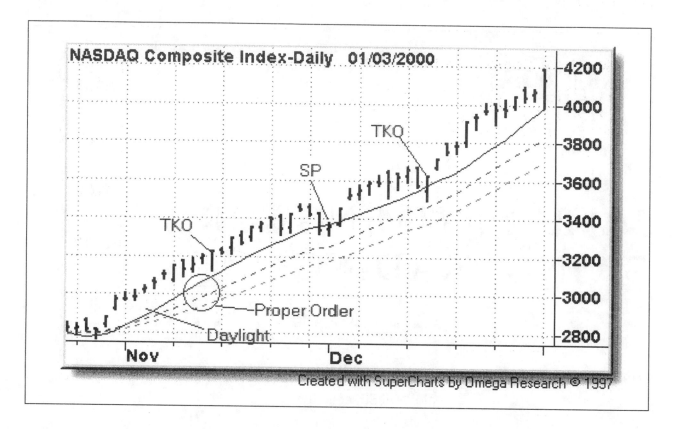

On the short side (Figure 10.2), notice that in the downtrend from March through May 2000, there were Trend Qualifiers, such as wide-range bars down, the moving averages had a negative slope, were in proper order for downtrends and there was Daylight between the highs and the moving averages. Also notice there were setups such as Bow Ties, Simple Pullbacks (SP) and Outside-Day Pullbacks (OD).

FIGURE 10.2

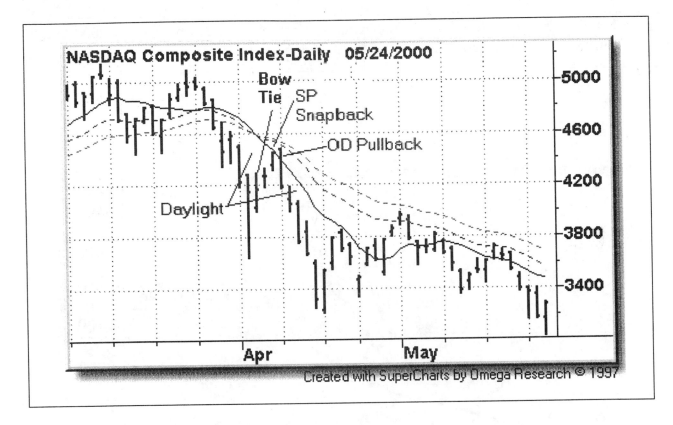

Continuing in my discretionary analysis, I also look at the 50-day simple and 200-day simple moving averages. I pay attention to these moving averages because they are well-watched by large institutions. In general, and unless I have some sort of other timing signal, I focus mostly on the long side when a market is trading above its 50-day and 200-day moving averages and focus mostly on the short side when the market is trading below its 50-day and 200-day moving averages. I also watch for a transition—that is, if a market is trading above both the 50 and 200 and then drops below the 50, I question whether or not a new downtrend is beginning or if it's simply a pullback.

Referring to Figure 10.3 below, notice that the Nasdaq traded well above its 50- and 200-day moving averages during its incredible run from October 1999 to March 2000. Also notice that the bear market of 2000 began with a sharp drop below the 50-day moving average (b).

FIGURE 10.3

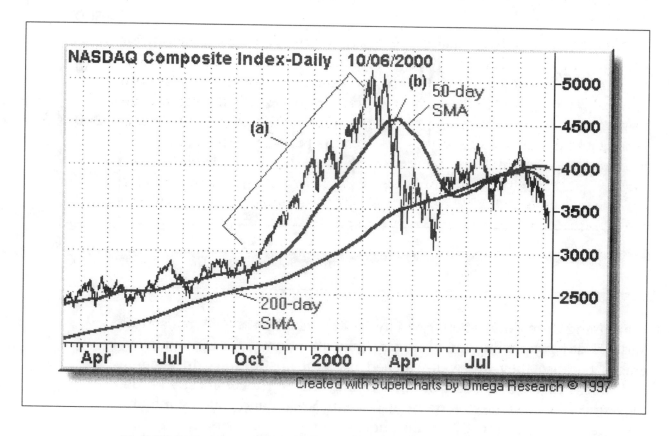

SYSTEM ANALYSIS

After completing my discretionary analysis, I then check to see if any systems based on market indicators may be triggering. The following three systems: The Oscillator Swing System, Trin Reversals and CVR III-Modified have historically shown a 60% to 70%-plus edge in predicting the stock market direction over the next three to seven days. Keep in mind that *I do not trade these systems in and of themselves on a mechanical basis.* Rather, I combine them with my discretionary analysis of the indices to help put me on the right side of the market when initiating swing trades.

OSCILLATOR SWING SYSTEM

The Oscillator Swing System (OSS) seeks to identify when the overall market is oversold (overbought) and seeks to go long (short) when the market has an intraday reversal. The system uses the 3-10 oscillator. This oscillator, popularized by Linda Raschke, co-author of *Street Smarts*, is simply a three-period simple moving average minus a 10-period moving average.

I define an "overbought" market as when the oscillator has gone up for five days in a row. Conversely, an "oversold" market is when the oscillator has gone down for five days in a row. I then look for an open-to-close reversal. That is, if the market is oversold, I look to see if the market can reverse intraday and close above its open. Finally, like all patterns in this book, I avoid taking trades *against* the trend. Therefore, if the market is in an uptrend, as defined by having an ADX reading of 30 or higher and +DMI > -DMI, shorts are not taken. Conversely, if the market is in a downtrend, as defined by having an ADX reading of 30 or higher and the –DMI > +DMI, then longs are not taken.

Here are the rules for the Oscillator Swing System:

For Buys

1. The market must *not* be in a downtrend, as defined by an ADX >= 30 and –DMI > +DMI.

2. The 3-10 oscillator must have at least five consecutive down days.

3. If the market closes *above* the open, go long on the close.

4. Exit on the close three to seven days later.

For Short Sales

1. The market must *not* be in an uptrend as defined by an ADX >= 30 and +DMI > –DMI.

2. The 3-10 oscillator must have at least five consecutive up days.

3. If the market closes *below* the open, go short on the close.

4. Exit on the close three to seven days later.

Let's look at an example before we review the results.

FIGURE 10.4

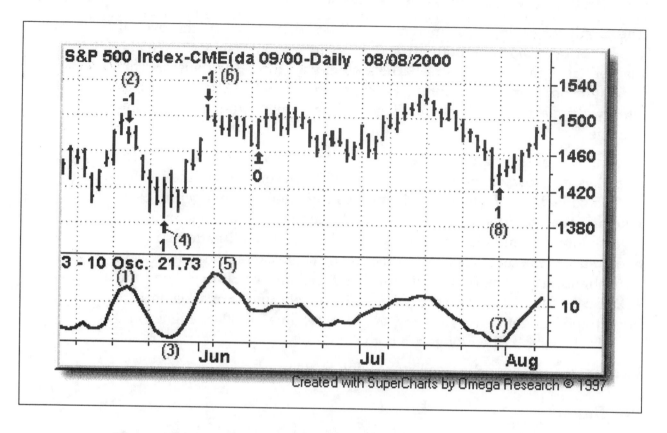

The ADX (not shown) in the June S&P futures is below 30, which suggests this market is not in a trend.

1. The 3-10 Oscillator of the September S&P futures rises for five consecutive days.

2. The contract closes below its open. Go short on the close.

3. Five consecutive days down in the 3-10 oscillator.

4. The market closes above the open. Go long on the close.

5. Five consecutive days up in the 3-10 oscillator.

6. The market closes below its open. Go short on close. Exit seven days later.

7. Five consecutive days down (ten total) in the 3-10 oscillator.

8. The contract closes above its open. Go long on the close. Exit seven days later.

Here are the results over the past ten years using a continuous S&P futures contract ($250 per point) and exiting on the seventh day. No stops or money management were used.

Notice that the short-side performance is much less than the long side. This reflects the longer-term bull market. Should we go into a prolonged downtrend, these numbers would likely reverse.

OSCILLATOR SWING SYSTEM: S&P 500 INDEX—CME-DAILY 01/05/1990–10/02/2000

Performance Summary: All Trades

Total net profit	$207900.00	Open position P/L	$0.00
Gross profit	$370587.50	Gross loss	−$162687.50
Total # of trades	143	Percent profitable	65%
Number winning trades	93	Number losing trades	50
Largest winning trade	$18575.00	Largest losing trade	−$20725.00
Average winning trade	$3984.81	Average losing trade	−$3253.75
Ratio avg win/avg loss	1.22	Avg trade (win & loss)	$1453.85
Max. consec. winners	10	Max. consec. losers	3
Avg # bars in winners	7	Avg # bars in losers	7
Max. intraday drawdown	−$38550.00		
Profit factor	2.28	Max. # contracts held	1
Account size required	$38550.00	Return on account	539%

Performance Summary: Long Trades

Total net profit	$167537.50	Open position P/L	$0.00
Gross profit	$259750.00	Gross loss	−$92212.50
Total # of trades	83	Percent profitable	71%
Number winning trades	59	Number losing trades	24
Largest winning trade	$18575.00	Largest losing trade	−$17975.00
Average winning trade	$4402.54	Average losing trade	−$3842.19
Ratio avg win/avg loss	1.15	Avg trade(win & loss)	$2018.52
Max consec. winners	9	Max consec. losers	2
Avg # bars in winners	7	Avg # bars in losers	7
Max intraday drawdown	−$38550.00		
Profit factor	2.82	Max # contracts held	1
Account size required	$38550.00	Return on account	435%

Performance Summary: Short Trades

Total net profit	$40362.50	Open position P/L	$0.00
Gross profit	$110837.50	Gross loss	−$70475.00
Total # of trades	60	Percent profitable	57%
Number winning trades	34	Number losing trades	26
Largest winning trade	$16075.00	Largest losing trade	−$20725.00
Average winning trade	$3259.93	Average losing trade	−$2710.58
Ratio avg win/avg loss	1.20	Avg trade(win & loss)	$672.71
Max consec. winners	6	Max consec. losers	5
Avg # bars in winners	7	Avg # bars in losers	7
Max intraday drawdown	−$25400.00		
Profit factor	1.57	Max # contracts held	1
Account size required	$25400.00	Return on account	159%

TRIN REVERSALS

In *Connors On Advanced Trading*, Larry Connors published his TRIN Thrusts strategy. This strategy seeks to go long when the NYSE TRIN indicator had a one-day thrust lower of 30% (or more) and seeks to go short when the TRIN had a one-day thrust of 30% or more higher. I found this system useful, especially when combined with other market indicators. However, in and of itself, I found the system generated too many signals for use in swing trading. Therefore, I decided to take the research one step further to find a TRIN-based system that would generate fewer signals and showed an edge geared more towards the swing trader—that is, one that would predict market direction over three to seven days. Larry originally published my research in the October 1998, issue of his *Professional Traders Journal*. Special thanks to Larry for allowing me to republish the system.

To those not familiar with the TRIN indicator, it was developed by Richard Arms in 1967 and was originally called the Arm's Index. The indicator is calculated by taking the ratio of Advancing Issues to Declining issues and dividing that by the ratio of advancing volume to declining volume. This formula is illustrated below.

$$\frac{\text{Advancing Issues / Declining Issues}}{\text{Advancing Volume / Declining Volume}}$$

If more volume is associated with advancing stocks than declining stocks, the TRIN will be less than 1.0. Conversely, if more volume is associated with declining stocks rather than advancing stocks, the TRIN will be greater than 1.00. Common Wall Street wisdom states that a TRIN reading above 1.00 suggests a market is oversold and due for a bounce and that a reading below 1.00 suggests a market is overbought and due to sell off. Be warned though, little money, if any, can be made by following "common Wall Street wisdom."

Rather than look for absolute levels of the average TRIN, I define an overbought market as when the three-day average of the TRIN is hitting 20- to 30-period lows and an oversold market as when the three-day average of the TRIN is hitting 20- to 30-period highs. As you likely know, just because a market is oversold doesn't mean it can't go lower. And, just because a market is overbought, doesn't mean it can't go higher. Therefore, once the three-day average of the TRIN is at one of these extremes, I then wait for the moving average of the TRIN to turn. This suggests that a major reversal has begun to take place from a market extreme.

Here are the rules for TRIN reversals:

For Buys:

1. The three-day simple moving average of the NYSE TRIN must make at least a 30-period high (shorter periods, say 20-period highs, will generate more but less accurate signals).

2. If today's three-day moving average of the TRIN is less than yesterday's (a "flip down" in the moving average) then buy the market on the close.

3. Exit three to seven days later.

For Short Sales:

1. The three-day simple moving average of the NYSE TRIN must make at least a 30-period low (shorter periods, say a 20-period low, will generate more but less accurate signals).

2. If today's three-day moving average of the TRIN is greater than yesterday's (a "flip up" in the moving average) then sell short the market on the close.

3. Exit (on the close) three to seven days later.

Here we have several back-to-back examples using the system to time the December 1999 S&P index futures.

FIGURE 10.5

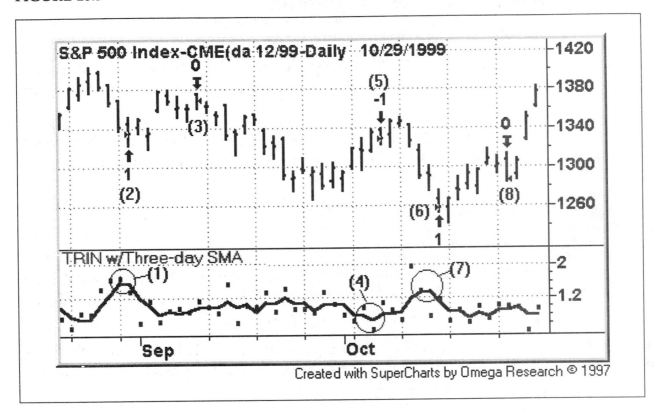

1. On 08/30/1999, the three-period moving average of the NYSE TRIN indicator makes a 30-period high. On 08/31/1999, the moving average turns down (today's average is less than yesterday's).

2. Buy the market on the close.

3. Exit on the close seven days later.

4. On 10/06/1999, the three-period moving average of the TRIN makes a 30-period low. On 10/07/1999, the moving average turns up.

5. Sell short the contract on the close.

6. Exit seven days later.

7. The same day, 10/15/1999, the TRIN average turns down after hitting a 30-period high, signaling a buy signal.

8. Exit seven days later.

Here are the results using a continuous S&P futures contract ($250 per point) over the last ten years. Exits were a fixed exit on the close of the seventh day. No stops or money management were used.

Notice that the system historically has had a better than 70% accuracy rate on the long side and also shows some promise on the short side by being historically 58% accurate. These numbers reflect the longer-term bull market and would likely reverse when we encounter a prolonged bear market.

TRIN REVERSALS S&P 500 INDEX—CME-DAILY 01/02/1990–10/02/2000

Performance Summary: All Trades

Total net profit	$201850.00	Open position P/L	$0.00
Gross profit	$358387.50	Gross loss	–$156537.50
Total # of trades	135	Percent profitable	(65%)
Number winning trades	88	Number losing trades	47
Largest winning trade	$35125.00	Largest losing trade	–$13100.00
Average winning trade	$4072.59	Average losing trade	–$3330.59
Ratio avg win/avg loss	1.22	Avg trade(win & loss)	$1495.19
Max consec. winners	9	Max consec. losers	4
Avg # bars in winners	7	Avg # bars in losers	7
Max intraday drawdown	–$23975.00		
Profit factor	2.29	Max # contracts held	1
Account size required	$23975.00	Return on account	842%

Performance Summary: Long Trades

Total net profit	$137712.50	Open position P/L	$0.00
Gross profit	$200475.00	Gross loss	–$62762.50
Total # of trades	73	Percent profitable	71%
Number winning trades	52	Number losing trades	21
Largest winning trade	$16375.00	Largest losing trade	–$7900.00
Average winning trade	$3855.29	Average losing trade	–$2988.69
Ratio avg win/avg loss	1.29	Avg trade(win & loss)	$1886.47
Max consec. winners	6	Max consec. losers	2
Avg # bars in winners	7	Avg # bars in losers	7
Max intraday drawdown	–$17675.00		
Profit factor	3.19	Max # contracts held	1
Account size required	$17675.00	Return on account	779%

Performance Summary: Short Trades

Total net profit	$64137.50	Open position P/L	–$0.00
Gross profit	$157912.50	Gross loss	–$93775.00
Total # of trades	62	Percent profitable	58%
Number winning trades	36	Number losing trades	26
Largest winning trade	$35125.00	Largest losing trade	–$13100.00
Average winning trade	$4386.46	Average losing trade	–$3606.73
Ratio avg win/avg loss	1.22	Avg trade(win & loss)	$1034.48
Max consec. winners	7	Max consec. losers	4
Avg # bars in winners	6	Avg # bars in losers	7
Max intraday drawdown	–$32800.00		
Profit factor	1.68	Max # contracts held	1
Account size required	$32800.00	Return on account	196%

CVR III—MODIFIED

The Chicago Board Options Exchange Volatility Index (VIX) measures the implied volatility (a measurement of cost) of the short-term (30 days) at-the-money OEX options. Market sell offs are normally associated with high VIX readings as panic drives the cost of these options higher. Conversely, during a gradual rising market, the VIX tends to drop as traders become complacent toward the market and option prices fall. Therefore, the VIX, in a sense, is a measurement of fear in the market. High readings (suggesting panic) normally occur near market bottoms and low readings (suggesting compliancy) normally occur near market tops. This makes the VIX a great contrary indicator.

Larry Connors, CEO of TradingMarkets.com, has done extensive research on using the VIX to predict short-term stock market moves. His Connors VIX Reversal (CVR) systems are based on the fact that volatility is mean (average) reverting. In other words, periods of higher-than-normal volatility are normally followed by lower or more average volatility. Conversely, periods of lower-than-normal volatility are normally followed by higher or more average periods of volatility. His CVR systems essentially look to position when the VIX reaches an extreme and begins to reverse

In 1997, while conducting research with Larry for *Connors On Advanced Trading,* Larry and I discovered that once the VIX was 10% or more away from its moving average, the stock market had a nearly 70% chance of reversing over the next three-to-seven days as the VIX returned to more average levels. Based on this research, we co-created the Connors VIX Reversal III (CVR III).

I've taken this research one step further and require that the VIX not only be at least 10% away from its moving average but must also reverse intraday. This suggests that the market is not only at an extreme but also has begun to reverse from that extreme. This "intraday reversal" is simply defined as the VIX closing below its open (suggesting volatility has begun to implode) for buys or for short sales, the VIX must close above its open (suggesting volatility has begun to increase).

Here are the rules for CVR III-Modified:

For Buys

1. Today, the low of the VIX must be *above* its 10-day moving average.

2. Today, the VIX must close at least 10% above its 10-day moving average.

3. Today, the VIX must close below its open.

4. Once rules 1 through 3 have been met, buy the market on the close.

5. Exit (on the close) the day the VIX trades (intraday) below yesterday's 10-day moving average (reversion to the mean).

For Short Sales

1. Today, the high of the VIX must be *below* its 10-day moving average.

2. Today, the VIX must close at least 10% *below* its 10-day moving average.

3. Today, the VIX must close *above* its open.

4. Once rules 1 through 3 have been met, sell short the market on the close.

5. Exit (on the close) the day the VIX trades (intraday) above yesterday's 10-day moving average (reversion to the mean).

FIGURE 10.6

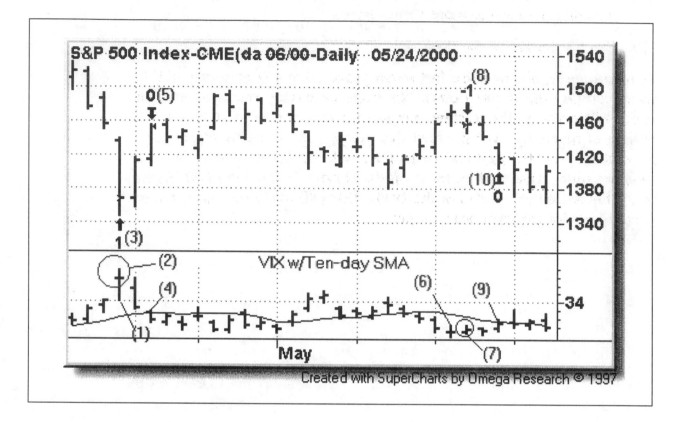

1. The low of the CBOE Volatility Index (VIX) is greater than its 10-day moving average.

2. The VIX closes below its open and its close is more than 10% above its 10-day moving average. This suggests the VIX has reached an extreme high and has begun to reverse.

3. Buy the market on the close.

4. The VIX trades back below its moving average suggesting that volatility has dropped to more normal levels.

5. Exit the market on the close.

6. The high of the VIX is below its 10-day moving average.

7. The VIX closes above its open and its close is more than 10% below its 10-day moving average. This suggests the VIX has reached an extreme low and has begun to reverse.

8. Go short on the close.

9. The VIX trades back to its 10-day moving averages, suggesting that volatility has risen to more normal levels.

10. Exit the market on the close.

Here are the results over the last seven years using a continuous S&P futures contract ($250 per point). No stops or money management was used. Historically, the system has shown that the market has a 76% chance of reversing over the next three days. Like virtually all mechanical systems over the past few years, the results on the long side (84% correct) are much greater than those on the short side (56% correct). Again, this reflects the bull market of the 1990s. This will likely reverse when we encounter a longer-term bear market.

CVR3-MODIFIED S&P 500 INDEX—CME-DAILY 04/26/1993–10/02/2000

Performance Summary: All Trades

Total net profit	$150512.50	Open position P/L	$0.00
Gross profit	$203750.00	Gross loss	−$53237.50
Total # of trades	63	Percent profitable	(76%)
Number winning trades	48	Number losing trades	15
Largest winning trade	$21300.00	Largest losing trade	−$19275.00
Average winning trade	$4244.79	Average losing trade	−$3549.17
Ratio avg win/avg loss	1.20	Avg trade (win & loss)	$2389.09
Max consec. winners	12	Max consec. losers	3
Avg # bars in winners	3	Avg # bars in losers	6
Max intraday drawdown	−$33175.00		
Profit factor	3.83	Max # contracts held	1
Account size required	$33175.00	Return on account	454%

Performance Summary: Long Trades

Total net profit	$105937.50	Open position P/L	$0.00
Gross profit	$146087.50	Gross loss	−$40150.00
Total # of trades	45	Percent profitable	84%
Number winning trades	38	Number losing trades	7
Largest winning trade	$21300.00	Largest losing trade	−$19275.00
Average winning trade	$3844.41	Average losing trade	−$5735.71
Ratio avg win/avg loss	0.67	Avg trade(win & loss)	$2354.17
Max consec. winners	10	Max consec. losers	1
Avg # bars in winners	3	Avg # bars in losers	7
Max intraday drawdown	−$28400.00		
Profit factor	3.64	Max # contracts held	1
Account size required	$28400.00	Return on account	373%

Performance Summary: Short Trades

Total net profit	$44575.00	Open position P/L	$0.00
Gross profit	$57662.50	Gross loss	−$13087.50
Total # of trades	18	Percent profitable	56%
Number winning trades	10	Number losing trades	8
Largest winning trade	$10800.00	Largest losing trade	−$5225.00
Average winning trade	$5766.25	Average losing trade	−$1635.94
Ratio avg win/avg loss	3.52	Avg trade (win & loss)	$2476.39
Max consec. winners	6	Max consec. losers	2
Avg # bars in winners	3	Avg # bars in losers	5
Max intraday drawdown	−$9825.00		
Profit factor	4.41	Max # contracts held	1
Account size required	$9825.00	Return on account	454%

WALK-THROUGH

Now that I have defined the steps I go through to gauge the overall market, let's walk through a period in early January 2000 when we had multiple buy signals.

FIGURE 10.7

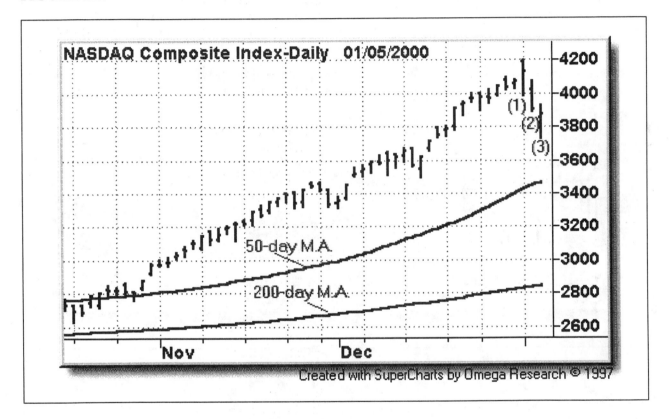

After trading well above its 50-day and 200-day moving averages for quite some time, the Nasdaq begins to correct. On January 5, 2000, the Nasdaq Composite forms a third back-to-back (1), (2), (3) Trend Knockout (TKO).

Looking to the S&P 500, I see that it has probed below its 50-day moving average but reversed and rallied to close right at the average.

FIGURE 10.8

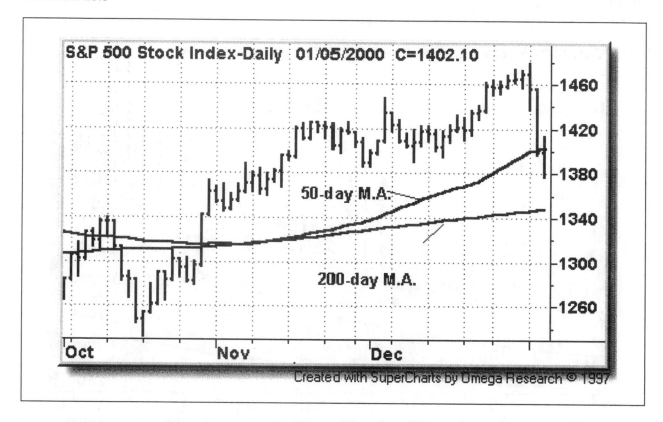

S&P 500 Stock Index-Daily 01/05/2000 C=1402.10

50-day M.A.

200-day M.A.

Oct   Nov   Dec

Created with SuperCharts by Omega Research © 1997

On the close of trading of 01/05/2000, a CVR III-Modified buy signal is
triggered.

FIGURE 10.9

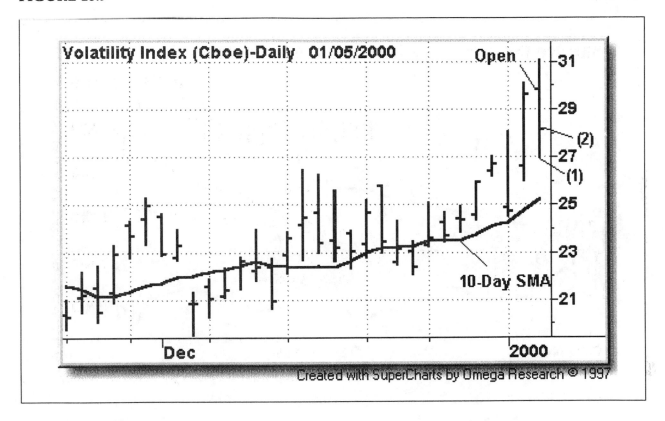

1. The low of the VIX is above its 10-day simple moving average.

2. The VIX closes 10% above the 10-day simple moving average (rule 2)
   and closes below its open (rule 3).

An Oscillator Swing System buy signal is also triggered on the close of 01/05/2000:

FIGURE 10.10

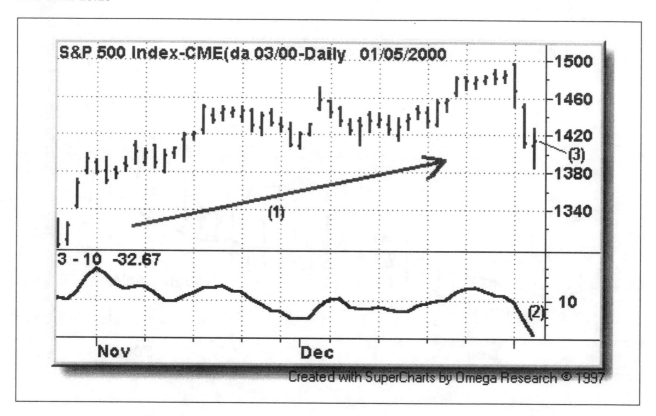

1. The S&P futures are not in a downtrend by a having low ADX reading of 18 (not shown).

2. The 3-10 oscillator drops for five consecutive days.

3. The S&P futures close above their open.

On 01/05/2000, the three-day average of the TRIN suggests that a buy signal is near:

FIGURE 10.11

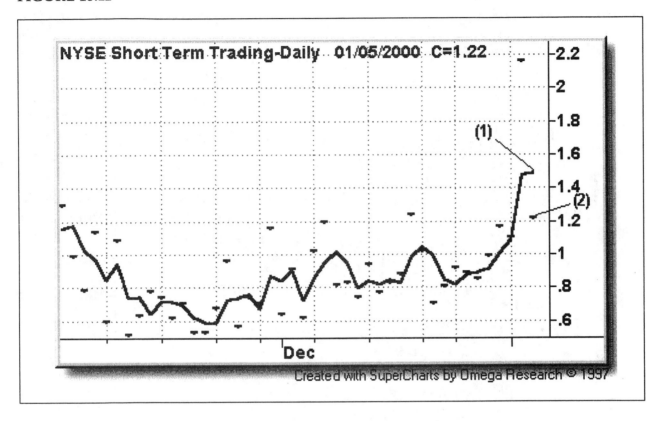

1. The three-day average of the TRIN hits a 30-day high.

2. The TRIN drops sharply, suggesting that we could get a buy signal (a flip down in the three-day average of the TRIN) within a day.

Now that we know the overall market is set up to rally, we take the next step and begin looking for the strongest sector(s).

FIGURE 10.12

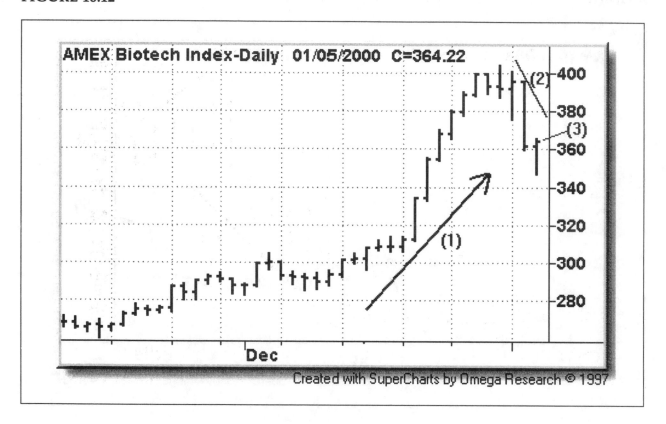

1. The AMEX Biotech Index (BTK) is in a strong uptrend.

2. The index has a sharp sell off.

3. On 01/05/2000, after probing lower, the index rallies to close well. This intraday reversal suggests the correction is over and the sector is poised to resume its strong uptrend.

Now that we have the overall market and sector behind us, we look for individual stocks in the sector that are set up.

FIGURE 10.13

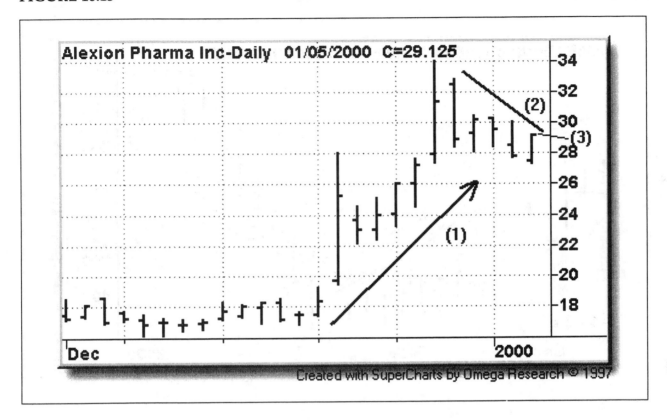

1. Alexion Pharmaceuticals (ALXN), a biotech, is in a strong uptrend.

2. The stock pulls back.

3. On 01/05/2000, after gapping lower, the stock reverses to close well. This intraday reversal suggests the correction is complete and the stock is poised to rally. We will look to go long tomorrow at 29 3/16, 1/16 above today's high.

Gilead Sciences (GILD), a biotech, sets up as a Bow Tie (Chapter 7).

FIGURE 10.14

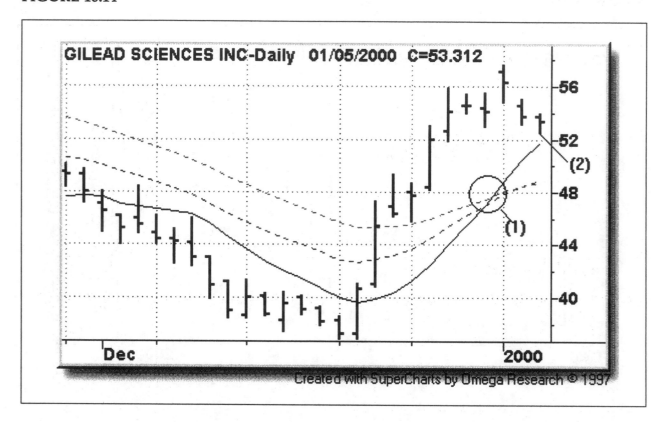

1. The moving averages converge and begin to spread out.

2. A lower low. We will look to go long tomorrow at 53 15/16, 1/16 above today's high.

On 01/05/2000, CV Therapeutics (CVTX) sets up as a Trend Pivot Pull-back and a low-volatility situation.

FIGURE 10.15

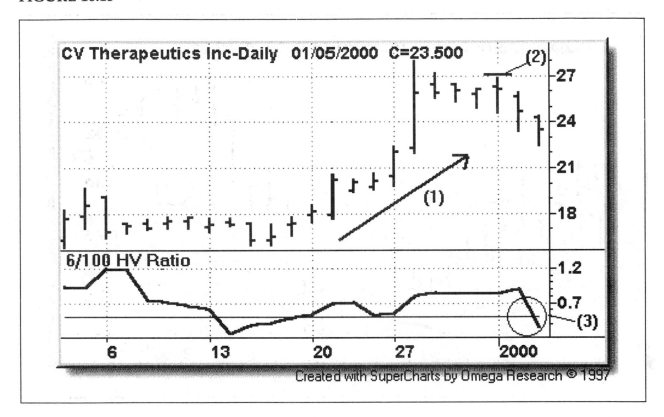

1. CVTX is in a strong uptrend.

2. The stock forms a Trend Pivot Pullback on 01/04/2000 (Chapter 6).

3. On 01/05/2000, the ratio of the 6/100 historical volatility drops below 50%, suggesting that a large move is imminent. We will look to go long tomorrow at 26 11/16, 1/16 above the pivot high (2).

On 1/6/2000 we get entries on CVTX, GILD and ALXN:

FIGURE 10.16

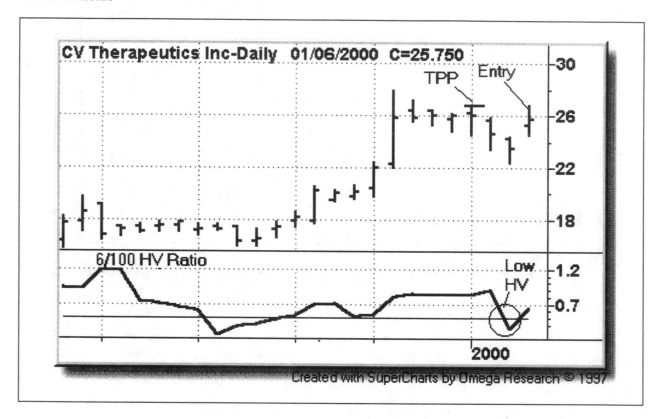

FIGURE 10.17

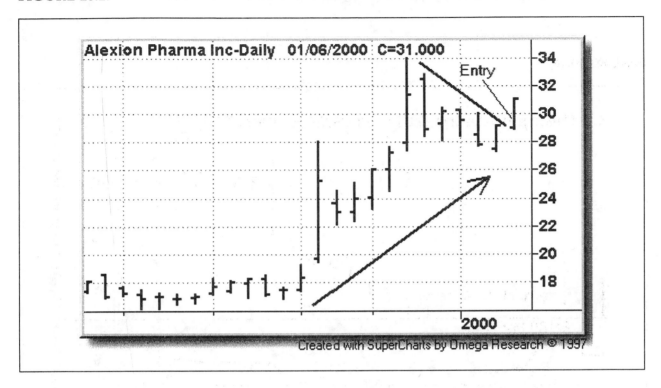

FIGURE 10.18

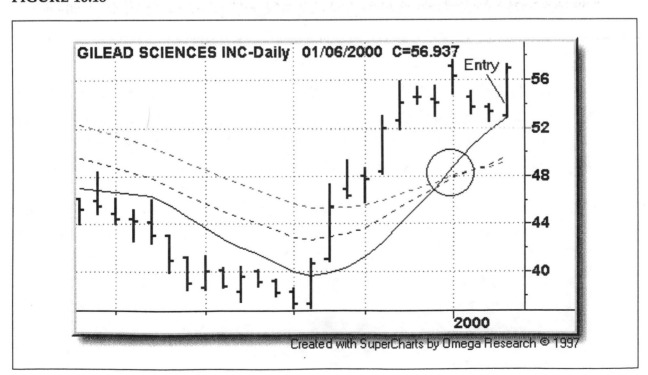

The entries are further confirmed (after the close) on 01/06/2000, by a buy signal in the Trin Reversal System.

FIGURE 10.19

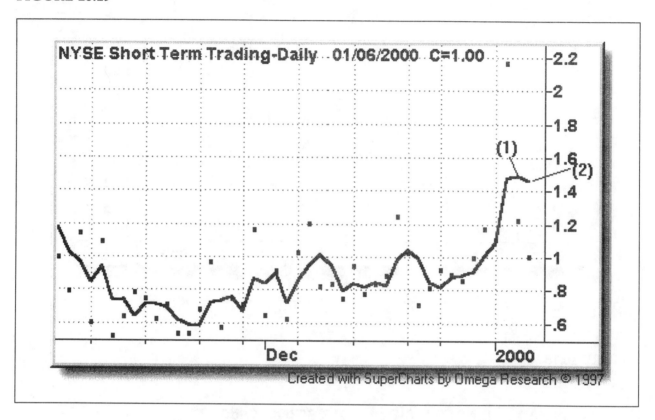

1. On 01/05/2000, the three-day average of the TRIN hits a 30-day high.

2. On 01/06/2000, the average "flips down" (today's average is less than yesterday's) signaling a buy signal in the Trin Reversal System.

Over the next few days, the S&P, Nasdaq, Biotech Index and the stocks that were set up: CVTX, GILD and ALXN all trade higher.

FIGURE 10.20

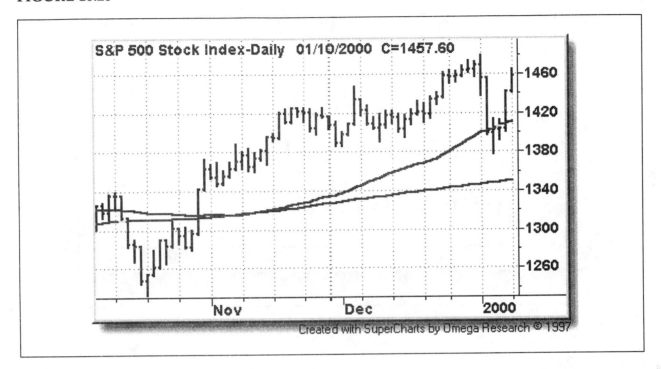

FIGURE 10.21

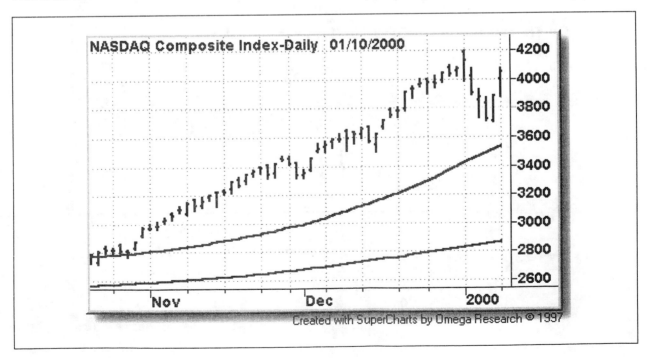

FIGURE 10.22

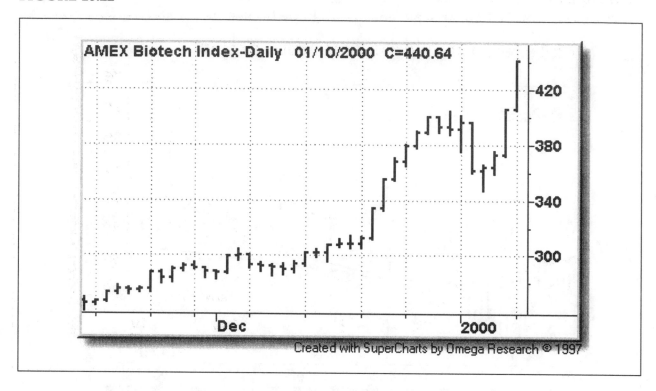

FIGURE 10.23

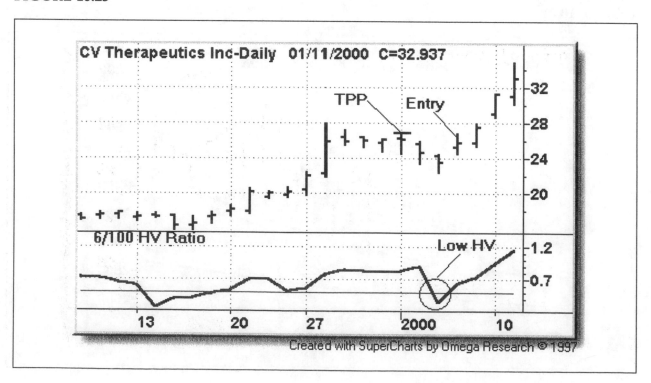

FIGURE 10.24

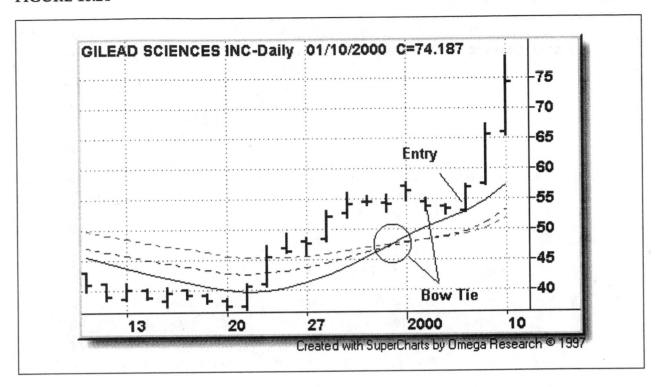

FIGURE 10.25

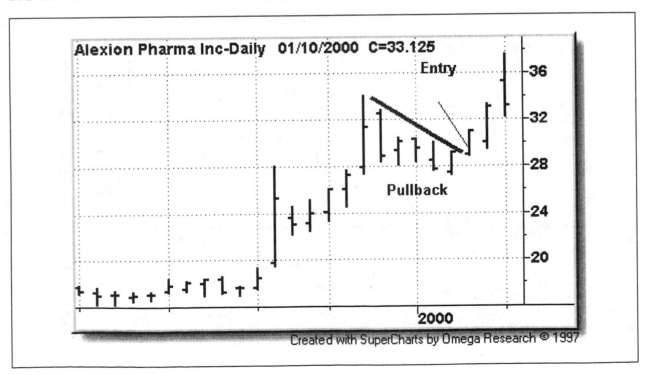

SUMMARY

As you can see, the odds are stacked in your favor as a swing trader by combining discretionary analysis, mechanical systems and sector analysis along with setups in individual issues.

Q&A

Q. Where can I find more information about the VIX indicator?

A. Contact the Chicago Board Options Exchange at www.cboe.com. Also, Connors VIX Reversal Signals are published nightly on TradingMarkets.com.

Q. Do you only trade when you have signals and setups in the indices/sectors such as those mentioned in your walk-through?

A. I'll trade as long as I have some sort of feel for the market. If I don't, then I'll take smaller position sizes. If these trades turn into losing positions, I may stop trading until I have a better feel for the markets. But, yes, ideally, I like to see systems kicking in along with patterns in the overall indices and sectors.

Q. In your walk-through, you had systems, patterns in the overall indices and sectors all occurring around the same time frame. During these times, do you tend to take larger positions sizes?

A. Yes, to some extent. There are only a few times a year when everything lines up. During these times, I may take a larger position size or possibly increase my leverage by taking an options trade. But, even though I know what the market *should* do, I keep risks in check just in case I'm wrong.

SECTION FIVE

OPTIONS

. . . .

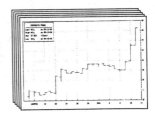

CHAPTER **11**

A FEW WORDS ABOUT USING OPTIONS WITH SWING TRADES

❑ ❑

The setups and concepts described in this manual are designed to capture explosive short-term moves in stocks. As such, they often lend themselves well to option trading. Be warned, however, options are an extremely complex vehicle and you must use utmost caution when trading them. Make sure you fully understand the nuances and risks involved. There are entire texts devoted strictly to option trading, pricing models and volatility. I strongly urge you to learn as much as possible about options before attempting to trade them.

It has been estimated that as much as 90% of those who trade options lose. Why? Because most who buy options do not have a strategy, a money-management plan in place, and tend to buy extremely speculative out-of-the-money options. The following guidelines, while by no means exhaustive, will help improve your odds when using options to initiate swing trades.

Avoid Out-of-the-Money Options—One of the main reasons most people lose when trading options is that they buy mostly out-of-the-money options. Although cheaper in absolute dollars, these options are normally very expensive in terms of true value. And more often than not, they expire worthless. Even if the underlying stock price rises sharply, these options often do not increase enough in value to make trading them worthwhile.

In order to avoid the pitfalls associated with out-of-the-money options, a good rule of thumb is to buy options that are 1 to 2 strikes *in the money*. These options will tend to trade in tandem with the underlying stock. For instance, if the stock rises 1 point in value, an in-the-money call option would also rise one point in value. In option lingo, this is known as having a delta of 100. This means the option trades in a similar manner to 100 shares of outright stock.

Buy the Nearby—As a swing trader we are looking to position ourselves for the next two to seven days. We do not have to increase our risk by buying longer-dated, higher premium options. Therefore, look to trade the front-month options unless the expiration is less than seven trading days away. In these cases, go to the following month's expiration.

Those familiar with options may argue that nearby options have worse time-decay profiles than longer-term options. I understand this argument, but believe that the potential of the patterns in this manual to make an immediate move far outweigh these drawbacks.

No Tickie, No Tradie—As discussed in Chapter 2, Landry's Rules and Money Management for the Swing Trader, you should not buy or sell short a stock unless it triggers a setup. The same holds true for buying options. Only buy options if, *and only if,* a setup triggers in the underlying stock. Be warned, however, if the stock is in a fast move when it triggers the setup, the spreads on the option will likely widen. In these cases you may have to be willing to forgo an options position.

Consider Options as a Stock Replacement on Profitable Stock Positions—Once a swing trade entry is triggered, in most cases, it's much easier to enter the underlying stock than it is to buy options. This is especially true during fast markets that often occur when setups are triggering. Therefore, you may want to consider options as stock replacement *after* you have entered the underlying stock and only if the position shows a reasonable profit.

For instance, if after entering a swing trade, you are fortunate enough to have a large profit, rather than carry a large stock position overnight, you might look to sell the position and buy options with a piece of your profits. This is, of course, provided the options are reasonably priced. This way, you have banked a profit and will still have the potential for a windfall profit on the option position with defined downside risk.

If You Hit a Double, Bank Half—Option prices often fluctuate wildly. Therefore, whenever you initiate an option position, you should immediately place a limit order to sell half of the position at twice your original cost. For instance, suppose you buy four options for $5 each, you would then place a limit order to two options at $10 (or slightly higher to cover commissions). Should the option spike higher, you'll get filled on this limit order and have covered the cost of the entire position. You should then look to scale out of these remaining options by following management principles outlined in this manual.

Q&A

Q.   You mentioned buying calls to replace stock in order to help reduce the risks of holding overnight. Why not just buy puts to hedge the position?

A.   You could but often the premium on the puts is often quite high because many with profits will be looking to hedge off risk. Also, if you buy puts, you now have to manage a hedge along with your original position. In other words, you have two positions to deal with. For instance, what if the stock continues to rise? You now have to buy higher strike puts in order to remained hedged. For me, it's easier to think and manage one position in one direction.

Q.   You don't mention option pricing models in your guidelines. Do you use them?

A.   As I said earlier, there are entire texts devoted strictly to option pricing models and volatility. My goal with this manual was to provide a complete manual for the stock trader. I do look at the implied volatility on the options and compare it to the historical volatility. I use this as a general guideline to gauge how expensive the option is. However, keep in mind that no option pricing model or technique can accurately predict future volatility. There are (albeit rare) times when options may appear expensive on the surface but are actually a bargain in reality.

Q.   Can you give us an example of when this occurs?

A. Sure, in a blow-off market, no one knows how far and how long it will go. For instance, in early 2000, call options were fairly priced but in reality, due to the extreme nature of the market, were actually cheap. Many at-the-money options became 10, 20, 30 or more points in the money in a matter of days. No option pricing model could have accurately predicted this.

Q. Do you have a favorite pattern for trading options?

A. The best setups are those that occur during a low-volatility situation (see Chapter 9, Finding Explosive Moves: An Advanced Lesson in Swing Trading). In these cases, option premiums tend to fall right before a large increase in volatility and stock price. This is the best of both worlds for the buyer of options.

Q, What about covered calls, spreads and other option strategies?

A. As mentioned earlier, the focus of this manual is predicting the short-term directional moves in stocks and not options trading. I prefer to keep it simple: I'll occasionally use calls if I'm bullish or puts if I'm bearish.

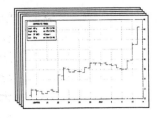

SECTION SIX

PSYCHOLOGY

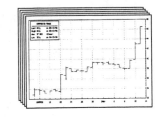

CHAPTER 12

TRADER'S PSYCHOLOGY

□ □

*The Speculator's chief enemies are
always boring from within.*

—Edwin LeFevre,
Reminiscences of a Stock Operator

*I'm afraid that some times
you'll play lonely games, too.
Games you can't win
'cause you'll play against you.*

—Dr. Seuss, *Oh! The Places You'll Go!*

In trading, there are many psychological barriers that you must overcome. The first step you must take is to realize that the trading world is much different than the "real world." For instance, in the "real world," as long as you perform your job to the degree expected of you, you'll continue to receive a paycheck on schedule. In trading, however, you can work hard, do everything "correct" and occasionally still lose money. Even worse, the markets will sometimes lull you into a false sense of security by rewarding "bad behavior" such as being careless and taking excessive risk.

In the real world if something goes awry on the job, it can be covered up, the blame can be shared and in some cases, insurance will cover the losses. In trading, however, there is no safety net and nowhere to hide. You must take responsibility for your actions. Your account balance doesn't lie.

In the real world, you are expected to stay busy. After all, they're not paying you to sit on your butt. In trading, however, sometimes the best thing to do is just that—nothing. Trying to make something happen in these environments can be detrimental to your account. The old saying, "Don't confuse activity with accomplishment" applies here.

Obviously, operating in the unstructured environment of the trading world versus the real world can be difficult. You have to manage yourself and your emotions. Below we will look at ways to recognize and overcome the psychological pitfalls of trading.

Realize That Losses Are Part of the Game—You can't take a loss personally. If you think about it, the guy on the other end of your trade has the exact opposite opinion of you. You can't both be right. Therefore, *every* trade has the potential to be a loser.

Money Management, Money Management, Money Management—Proper money management will help solve many of the psychological pitfalls of trading. For instance, if you are only risking 1% to 2% per trade, then any individual loss should be of little consequence.

Have Confidence—You must be comfortable with your methodologies. You develop this comfort through historical research, real-time observation and trading. This does not mean that you are confident to the point that you are infallible on any one trade. Rather, you know that through a consistent approach, you will make money in the long run.

Remain Humble—This may seem like a contradiction to confidence but a good trader must also be humble. The best traders are confident about their methods but humbled by the fact that market can do anything it wants in spite of their opinions.

Realize That You Have No Control Over the Markets—The market can do whatever it wants. It is made up of millions of individuals who you have absolutely no control over. The best setup in the world won't work if some hedge fund or large trader decides to dump his position (for whatever reason) right after you enter the market. Also, you have no control over outside influences. This doesn't have to be something obvious like a war or even an off-the-cuff remark from a world leader. It can be something as simple as the actions of some lunatic. For example, I once was knocked out of a perfectly good and profitable S&P futures trade because some psychopath decided to start shooting people in our nation's capital building.

Forget About Being Right—In swing trading as many as half of your trades will result in a loss. Yet through controlling those losses, the winning trades will more than make up for the other half. Your goal is not to be right. Your goal is to make money, period.

Realize That No Methods Are Perfect—Be a student of the markets but realize that there is no "Holy Grail"—an infallible system that will lead to riches without risk. Stick with simple conceptually correct methods such as those outlined in this manual. In the past, many have made billions on simple systems such as those developed by Donchian. In his words: *"In this field of technical study, it is probably safe to state that the beginning of wisdom comes when you stop chasing rainbows and admit that no method is perfect. When you find yourself willing to settle for any comparatively simple method that, in tests over a long period, makes money on balance, then stick to the method devotedly, at least until you are sure that you haven't discovered a better method."*

Be Consistent—You must be consistent in your approach to the markets. You will never be successful as long as you are jumping from method to method. Find something that works and stick to it.

Keep Emotions in Check—Those who become euphoric when things are good are also those how tend to fall the hardest things turn bad. Strive to stay on an even keel in good times and bad.

> *In Times Of War Prepare For Peace*
> *In Times Of Peace, Prepare For War*
>
> —Sun Tzu

In good times, you must realize that you are just around the corner from a string of losses. Conversely, after a string of losses, better times often follow.

Embrace Who You Are—We are all individuals with our own psychological makeup. Recognize and embrace what makes you different and use it to your favor when trading. For instance, I was raised with a strong work ethic. Phrases such as "There's no free lunch" were common in my household when I was growing up. However, as mentioned previously, sometimes in trading, the best thing to do is nothing. This goes completely against my upbringing. At these times I would feel lazy and guilty for "not working." I would then try to make something happen by establishing positions even though I knew I shouldn't. I finally realized that during poor market conditions, I must channel my energy into something other than trading. I've discovered that if I used this time to conduct market research, I felt productive without having to expose my equity unnecessarily.

Treat Profits as Your Own Money—Chances are, if you are a successful trader, you have worked very hard to achieve this goal. Therefore, when you make money trading, you are being paid for that hard work. It's your money and should be treated no differently than a paycheck. Do not become careless and violate your rules because it is the "market's money" or a "free" position. It's ok to *occasionally* press a little when you have windfall profits, just make sure you keep the lion's share.

Only Trade When You Are Of Sound Body And Mind—Do not trade around major life events or when you are sick, distracted or simply not prepared.

Only Trade When You Have an Edge—The best times to trade are the times when the overall market and individual sector(s) are suggesting a clear direction. It is at these times you will find yourself having trouble choosing between all those wonderful setups. Other times, when its extremely difficult to determine market and sector direction, it will be nearly impossible to find decent setups. And when you do, you'll often find yourself quickly stopped out. At these times, you must be patient and wait for better times.

Be Positive in Life But Skeptical in the Markets—In life, we are taught to be positive. "Look on the bright side," "Things normally work out" and "Have faith" are phrases we have all heard over and over. However, having faith and hope for a losing position is fruitless. The best traders don't focus on what they will make on a trade but rather how much they can lose and how to manage that risk. Successful traders are positive in life and confident that their methodologies will work over the long haul but remain skeptical on any given trade.

Don't Expect Immediate Success—Some of the worst novice traders I know are medical doctors. Why? Because they are successful in what they do and automatically assume they can transfer their success to trading. They forget that it took an intense study of 10 years before they were allowed to cut on their first patient.

My intent is not to pick on doctors, I also know incredibly successful lawyers, engineers and even a rocket scientist that think that they can quickly pick up trading because they have become masters in their careers. What they fail to remember is that it took them more than a few weeks to become successful in their professions.

Learn from Your Losses—A loss in the market is not a total loss as long as something is learned. For instance, after getting stopped out numerous times only to watch the trend resume, I discovered the Trend Knockout (TKO) (Chapter 6).

Work Hard and Love What You Do—You should be passionate about trading. It is not something you should do casually. Because money is the ultimate motivator, I can assure you those on the other sides of your trades have dedicated the better part of their lives to trading. And, they are all too happy to take money away from those less serious.

Keep a Journal—Other than finding a methodology that makes sense to you and applying strict money-management principles, the best way to become a better trader is to monitor yourself and your own performance. I strongly urge to you keep a trading journal. Whenever you enter a trade you should write: What motivated it? What was the setup? What is the overall market doing? What is the sector of the stock doing? If the trade is a larger- (or smaller-) than-normal position size, why? Print and label any charts that support you claim. Once all the mechanics are down, make sure you include a little about yourself. Are you feeling well? Are their any stresses weighting you down? Have you experienced any major life changes recently? Have you been making money lately?

Plot Your Equity—The value of your trading account does not lie. If you made it this far in this manual then by now you should know what a trend is. Therefore, if your equity curve is trending steadily higher, then you are doing something right and/or market conditions are favorable. On the other hand, if your equity curve is trending lower, then you are doing something wrong and/or market conditions are unfavorable. Stop trading and reevaluate the situation with a clear head. The name of the game is long-term survival. The markets will always be there.

I know several traders who know very little about market timing, yet are always out of the markets when conditions are at their worse. How? They stop trading after a string of losses, wait for better times and then slowly ease back in.

Reflect At the end of the day, take a few minutes to quietly reflect on your trading. Mentally rehash the day's events. What did you do right? What did you do wrong? What could you have done better? Did you keep losses in check? Did you honor your stops? Did you take partial profits if they were offered to you?

SUMMARY

The trading world is vastly different from the real world. There are many psychological barriers that must be overcome. However, if you strive to become successful, I can assure you that it will be well worth the effort. With hard work and devotion, there is no limit to what you can achieve. Think about it. How many times at work have your accomplishments gone unnoticed and un-rewarded? How many times have others taken credit for your actions? This will *never* happen in the trading world. You *and only you* control your own destiny.

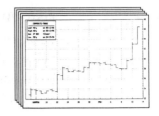

CHAPTER **13**

LESSONS LEARNED

∎ ∎

Over the years, I have learned many lessons about trading through the school of hard knocks. In more recent times, by being a public figure in the trading world, I have been able to re-learn these and new lessons through fellow traders. The following are some of my favorites.

START TRAINING ON MONDAY, COMPETE ON WEDNESDAY

My wife Marcy asked me if I would discuss trading with two of her clients and their spouses. She explained to me that they are all going to plop down $3,000 dollars each on a weekend seminar that would teach them "everything they needed to know to immediately start earning a living trading." Marcy knew that none of these individuals had every traded and feared the seminar would be a waste of their money. And worse, she was concerned that they would lose much more money should they decide to jump into the markets. I agreed and we all had dinner the following Sunday night.

After patiently listing to a regurgitation of the motivational speech that had been given to them, I studied the materials that were to be covered. To my surprise, it involved technical analysis and didn't involve any "magic" systems. However, much of the material was dated and wasn't anything you couldn't get from a good $50 primer on the subject. Furthermore, it certainly wasn't enough for a novice to become a full-time trader a few days later.

I tried to talk them out of the seminar in several different ways. I offered to loan them books, suggested they get a free trial to TradingMarkets.com and even was willing to give them private lessons for free—provided of course they were serious about learning. I emphasized that they should do this *before* plopping down money on a get-rich seminar. All of this fell on deaf ears as they once again repeated the sales pitch to me.

As I watched them drink their water and eat their bland chicken and vegetables, finally it hit me, I had to speak in their terms. The gentlemen were body builders and their wives were fitness fanatics. All had the utmost discipline and had been training for years. One of the men held several regional bodybuilding titles and the other was preparing to compete in his first amateur competition. For dramatic effect, I put a whole jumbo shrimp into my mouth, took a big slurp of my 25-ounce beer and slammed it down on the table. Talking with my mouth full, I then said, "You know what? I'm going to finish this beer, my fried shrimp appetizer, my 14-ounce steak and fries and on Monday I'm going to start training and dieting (I was about 30 pounds overweight at the time). Then, on Wednesday, I'm going to compete in a bodybuilding contest."

Follow-Up: Couple A heeded my advice and avoided the seminar. Instead, they continued to focus on growing the business they owned. In fact, the business has grown so much that they have recently considered franchising.

Couple B attended the seminar, quit their jobs, and after a brief stint at trading, are now searching for the next get-rich-quick scheme.

The moral: Becoming a successful trader is possible, but it takes more than a weekend.

ENJOY THE RIDE

Joe is a successful long-term trader who decided to try his hand at swing trading. I began working with Joe and he became quite successful in a short period of time. The fact that he started during the greatest bull market blow off in last 20 years didn't hurt either.

One day we were discussing the markets and he said that he had already made over $35,000 and it wasn't even noon. He was bragging that this just about covered his tricked-out sport-utility vehicle that he had ordered the day before. At this point, I told him, "As soon you hang up the phone, cash out, write a check and pay for your new truck." Then, no matter what happens to you in the markets, at least you have nice truck to ride around in. He took my advice and paid cash for his truck.

Follow-up: Ironically, Joe suffered a severe loss in the markets in the following few weeks but is really enjoying his SUV.

The moral: Take something out.

NURSING POSITIONS

Longer term, Bill was a successful trader but had recently entered some bad trades. We were talking one day about all the setups there were. I assumed that he must be printing money as we were both looking at the same stocks and they were all moving nicely. When I inquired about his position size, he replied that he did not take these new positions because he was too busy "nursing all his bad positions."

The moral? Because he was focused on positions that were not working, he missed all the opportunity of the new stocks that were setting up. To quote Livermore, "The chap who is compelled to lug a corpse a year or two always loses more than the original cost of the deceased; he is sure to find himself tied up with it when some really good things come his way."

WHO MAKES A BETTER TRADER: AN MBA OR A RECEPTIONIST?

Many years ago, I worked on a base where they used to test rocket engines. The base was so large that it had its own fitness facility. One day, I walked into the gym with a long face.

The receptionist: "What's wrong?"

Me: "I'm in a bunch of bad stocks."

The receptionist: (with a perky little smile and a high-pitched bouncy voice): "Well, sell them and buy a bunch of good stocks."

Her statement infuriated me. After all, I had recently completed my MBA and had been studying the market for a few years. I thought, "What the hell does a receptionist know about trading?"

Follow-Up: Evidently, she knew a lot more about trading than I did at that time. Taking this simple advice would have saved me about $30,000—a lot of money for a kid fresh out of school!

The moral: Trading is not rocket science.

THE GENIUS

Mike, an accomplished long-term trader, has recently begun swing trading. He calls me a few times a week. Almost always, it's the same conversation:

Mike: "I'm up 4 points on XYZ, what should I do? "

Me: "Sell half and move your stop on your remaining shares to breakeven."

Mike: "Man, that's great advice. You're a genius!"

The moral: Simple money management is not rocket science.

NEVER-WRONG MAN

Never-Wrong Man never loses money trading. Even when he's following a mechanical system, he "forgets" to take the losing trades. There's always an excuse. "I got busy and forgot to check my signals." Or "the broker screwed my order up, so while I thought I was losing money, in reality the trade didn't go through." When he does take what would turn out to be a losing trade, there's always another excuse. For instance, "you know, I can't explain it, but I just decided to sell the stock afterhours, five minutes before the bad news came out."

I used to be intimidated by Never-Wrong Man. I would think, "Geez, what's wrong with me? Why do I make mistakes? Take bad trades? Get stopped out? Why can't I be more like Never-Wrong Man?" I later realized that no one is immune to losses in this game, not even Never Wrong Man. You win some, you lose some and hopefully, by being consistent and controlling losses, you make money overall.

The moral: Big Foot, The Loch Ness Monster and Never-Wrong Man allegedly exist, yet their existence has yet to be proved.

ANTHILL

Bob entered a swing trade and failed to place a protective stop. Within hours, he was down over 20 points. The next day, he got an incredible break, the stock came all the way back plus some. Bob was smug about his trade as cashed out for a 2-point gain.

The moral: Mark Boucher refers to a strategy like Bob's as an "Anthill" strategy: Ants can build a significant mound with tiny little bits and pieces but all it takes is one big footprint to smash it down.

METHOD MAN

Method Man is a setup junkie. He reads everything he can get his hands on regarding trading. The problem is, he runs out and tries to apply concepts with his hard-earned money literally minutes after reading about them. He doesn't take the time to do the proper research, to prove that the setup has worked historically and through real-time observation. Method Man *occasionally* gets lucky but never has consistent longer-term performance.

The moral: Find something that works and stick to it.

SHOW-AND-PULL

I once checked out a chat room full of daytraders just to see what it was all about. There were a few smaller "wannabes" in the room, but for the most part, it was made up of larger, well-capitalized traders. One of the newer traders entered a small position in a thinly traded stock. The stock looked impressive and fit all the criteria for a good setup. After mentioning the stock to the group and the fact he was long 100 shares, one of the larger traders in the group decided to have a little fun. He said, "Hey, everyone, pull up XYZ on your Level II quote screens...now watch this..." He then put out a 10,000-share offer on the stock. He laughed as the smaller began to squirm and beg him to take it down. A few seconds later, he removed the offer.

Now here's a guy that was screwing around just to get a few laughs. However, this could have had a material impact on the stock. What if other traders would have been scared out of their position based on this bogus offer? A chain reaction could have knocked the small trader out of a perfectly good position.

The moral: All it takes is one jerk to screw up a perfectly good trade.

GET YOURSELF A PUNCHING BAG

Steve, a daytrader, always had a chip on his shoulder. He was constantly mad at the market makers for "screwing him." In fact, on some days, Steve would send me numerous emails complaining about the above. He would even go through the painstaking process of providing time and sales information and other information to support his claims. He became so obsessed he began watching stocks that he had no intention of trading just so he could prove his point. I couldn't image where an active daytrader was finding so much time intraday. I knew he had to be missing numerous opportunities while expending all that negative energy. Finally, after getting tired of reading all his emails, I decided to take action. I explained to him that he was wasting far too much energy on things he couldn't control. Further, I admitted that I, too, occasionally got mad at brokers, market makers and the market in general but instead of obsessing over it, I go to the back of my office and beat on my punching bag. After a few minutes of this, I return to my screens focused and refreshed. Next!

The moral: Get yourself a punching bag.

RETIRE ON A SAILBOAT

John, a friend of mine, became incredibly bullish on a certain stock. Starting with $5,000, he began buying options on the stock. Turns out, John's analysis was right. The options soon became worth many thousands of dollars. As the options neared expiration, he sold them and parlayed the money into more further out-of-the-money options. He began to repeat this process over and over. This strategy was so successful that he quit his day job. As he approached the million-dollar mark, I suggested that he lock in his profits and place them into a secure fixed-income investment. He explained to me that when he reached four million he was going to buy a sailboat and retire.

Follow-Up: Unfortunately, the stock began to implode soon after he reached a million dollars. His entire account was wiped out over the next few weeks.

The moral: Don't expect the market to fulfill your dreams. To quote Livermore: "There isn't a man on Wall Street who has not lost money trying to make the market pay for an automobile or a bracelet or a motor boat or a painting."

THE BEAR HAS EYES

In the late '90s during one of the greatest bull markets in history, Bear Man, one of the best daytraders in the world, was constantly faxing, emailing and calling me to talk about how the bull market was coming to an end. He'd support his claims with articles and newsletters along with market statistics and historical comparisons. His research was often thorough and quite convincing

The conversations were almost always the same. After about 10 minutes of listening to his bearish arguments:

Me: "Okay, I know you are bearish. So what are you trading?"

BM: "I'm long, ABC, CDE and EFG."

Me: "Why no shorts?"

BM: "Because the market is going up."

The moral: Bear Man never confuses being right with making money. This is *why* he is one of the greatest traders in the world.

OH, I DON'T LIKE TO TAKE A LOSS

After just a few months of trading, Mike had become a very successful trader. In fact, he was so successful that he was on the verge of shutting down his successful law practice so he could focus on trading. Impressed (and somewhat envious) with his immediate success, I inquired about his methods. He told me that he buys the hottest stocks on the momentum lists. When I asked about his risk control, he stated, "Oh, I don't like to take a loss . . . they'll come back."

Follow-Up: I can't say for sure that Mike has been wiped out, but I do know that his law practice has been dissolved and he appears to have vanished off the face of the earth. I hope the best for Mike but fear the worst.

The moral: Use a stop.

IMPRESS YOUR FRIENDS

John was lucky enough to pick a hot Genomic stock as his first trade. The stock shot up from 20 to 70 in a few days. When I asked him how he was going to exit, he replied "I'm going to wait until it hits 300 so I can tell my friends I was in it at 20." A few days later, the stock imploded and was trading below his entry.

The moral: If you want to really impress your friends, throw a party and spring for the beer.

BALANCE

Sharon achieved the success that many aspiring traders dream of. In a short period of time she amassed a small fortune through her trading. This was not done through pure luck alone. She studied the markets morning, noon and night. She did not take trading casually, it was her life. In fact, she worked so hard that it was beginning to cause problems with her home life. She finally had to decide between trading and her family. She realized that if she chose trading, eventually the tremendous psychological burden from her family would hurt her performance. She chose her family and placed most of her profits with a professional money manager with a long-term track record.

The moral: Work hard but balance your life.

I'M THE KING OF THE WORLD

In late February of 2000, I was having my best year ever in my private trading. I was up several hundred percent in nearly all of my accounts. Further, my ego was being fed by the readers of my TradingMarkets.com stock column. They were sending me emails praising my stock-picking abilities. On top of all this, my wife was scheduled to deliver my first child in a few weeks. I felt bulletproof and invincible, kind of like Leonardo DiCaprio's character on the front of the *Titanic*. Jeff Cooper warned me that it wasn't a good idea to trade around major life events. He suggested that I bank profits and take a break for a while. Unfortunately, I didn't heed his advice. I continued to trade actively. In fact, I was even placing trades from the delivery room in-between my wife's contractions. Ironically, my daughter, Isabelle Florence, was born minutes after the Nasdaq closed above 5,000 for the first time in history. As I held her up to the CNBC screen for my bragging pictures, I remember thinking that, at the rate I was going, I would have her college paid for within the next few weeks. I was invincible.

Follow-Up: My accounts peaked the same day my daughter was born. Although I was able to stay in the black, I gave up a significant portion of the profits over the next month or so.

The moral: The "king of the world" eventually went down on the *Titanic*. Keep your ego in check and don't trade around major life events.

SECTION SEVEN

PUTTING THE
PIECES TOGETHER

. . . .

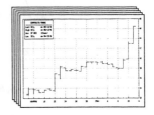

CHAPTER **14**

NIGHTLY PREPARATION

□ □

If people only knew how hard I worked to gain my mastery,
it wouldn't seem so wonderful at all.

—Michelangelo Buonarroti

As I stated in Trader's Psychology, money is the ultimate motivator. As such, it attracts some of the brightest minds in the world. I can assure you those on the other sides of your trades are prepared. And they are all too happy to take your money away from you if you are not. The following is how I prepare for the next trading day. It's a lot of work, but for me it's like being on a treasure hunt.

POSTMORTEM

Right after the market closes, I take a few minutes to review and reconcile the day's trades and plot my equity. I then find a quiet place and spend 5–10 minutes mentally reviewing the day's actions. As mentioned in Trader's Psychology, it is at this time I think about what trades were taken and why, what went right, what went wrong, what could I have done better and so on and so forth. I then make the appropriate notes in my trading journal.

ANALYZE A SMALL DATABASE

I keep a small database of 400-600 stocks that I download shortly after the close. The database contains the bellwether and popular stocks such as Intel and Microsoft, the 30 Dow Jones Industrial Average stocks, many tech issues from the Nasdaq 100, a few cyclicals such as oils and oil service and representative stocks from a variety of sectors. The above makes up the core database and it rarely changes. The remainder of the database is made up of momentum stocks and the current "glamour" stocks. I cull these out as they drop below certain levels (usually $10 per share) or lose momentum. New stocks for the database are found by going through momentum lists, such as the TradingMarkets.com Proprietary Momentum (and Implosion) lists, TradingMarkets.com StockScanner, talking with other traders, stocks mentioned on CNBC and any other stocks I find in my nightly analysis. This database grows and shrinks as various sectors heat up and cool off.

My charting software allows me to "click" through each and every chart in this database. On average, I spend between 2-3 seconds on each chart. Even though I have scanning software to scan for most of the patterns listed in this manual (more on this below), I still like to look through the charts because it gives me a feel for what's going on in the markets. Sometimes I can pick up on "themes" that cannot be found via computer-based scans or through overall sector analysis. For instance, I might notice some "hidden" aspects, such as pockets of strength in otherwise down sectors, or "old tech," or under-performing "new tech."

In going through the charts, I'll also stop and analyze any chart that made a large move for the day. I then ask myself, could I have predicted this ahead of time? Is it one of my patterns? Is it possibly a new pattern?

The exercise of actually going through all of these charts (vs. relying solely on the computer scans) not only unearths potential for the next trading day, it also makes me a better chart reader. It's no different than a musician practicing.

ANALYZE SPECIALIZED DATABASES

Depending on market conditions, I often keep separate small databases for specific sectors. For instance, in late 1999/early 2000, the Genomic stocks were on fire. Therefore, during such periods, I'll keep a completely separate database of only these stocks. This helps to me to focus on the hottest stocks in the hottest sectors. Obviously, these databases change with the times. They range from the complete sector such as telecommunications down to a specific niche within that sector (e.g., fiber optics).

ANALYZE IPOS

I also keep a small database of the Initial Public Offerings (IPOs) that went public over the last three months. These can be found through Internet sources such as TradingMarkets.com and IPO.com. Often these newer stocks offer great swing-trade setups as the euphoria over the promise outweighs the reality. As nimble swing traders, we can often capture a piece of these moves before that reality sets in.

SECTOR ANALYSIS

After completing my analysis of the above databases, I then look through the main sector charts such as the semiconductors, banks, biotech, oil service, major drugs, gold and silver, broker/dealer, telecommunications, etc. I look for setups in these sectors, bigger-picture patterns and momentum in general.

OVERALL MARKET ANALYSIS

I then look at what the overall indices are doing. This analysis was covered in detail under Chapter 10, Market Timing for Swing Trading.

STUDY FUTURES MARKETS

I download and analyze about 30 active futures markets. Even if you don't intend on trading futures, it's a good idea to know what's going on here because markets don't exist in a vacuum. For my stock swing trading, I pay careful attention to what's going on in the index futures and the bond market. I'll also analyze what's going on in the currency markets and commodities in general (e.g., crude oil).

ANALYZE SCANS

All of the above takes between one-and-a-half and two hours. During this time, I have scans running on my main database of over 5,000 active stocks. These scans give me pullbacks, Double Top Knockouts, Bow Ties and most of the other patterns and concepts outlined in this manual.

I also look at of the stocks produced by TradingMarkets.com indicators. Not only does this provide me with potential setups, but it also may give me themes that I might not have picked up on through my own analysis and scans. Further, it also often provides me with stocks that may be worth watching for setups over the next few days.

FINAL PREP

I then take all of the above analysis and put together my game plan. I make a list of the stocks I want to watch for the following day. I also check to see if they are optionable, make specific notes about where I should enter and where my protective stops should be placed. I plug the stocks into my quote screen and set alarms *near* the trigger points. Finally, I check the after hours index futures for any late-breaking news that could throw a wrench in any of my analysis.

When I arrive at my office the next morning, I have a game plan in front of me and my screens are ready to go. There's no last-minute stress or scrambling involved with not being prepared. I sip my coffee and wait for the opening.

Q&A

Q.   You mentioned only spending 2-3 seconds per chart while tooling through your small database of up to 600 stocks. What can be gathered in such a small amount of time?

A.   A time of 2-3 seconds is only an average. If I don't like a chart, I might only spend a fraction of a second on it. On others, I might spend a minute or longer or make a note to come back to it later.

Q.   How do you know to only spend a "fraction of a second on a chart"?

A.   After a while you begin to memorize the charts. For instance, I know that XYZ has been trading in a low-level base for months. When I get to this chart, unless the chart is showing some signs of life, I think, oh, that's XYZ, I see it's still in the toilet. Next!

Q.   Why not rely solely on the scans?

A.   Most people are looking for the easy way out. And the scans do a wonderful job of reducing the workload and finding setups. However, looking at charts gives you a much better picture of what's going on under the surface.

Q.   Why look at so many charts?

A.   I'm a technician. And, technicians predict the markets through the use of charts. The more charts I look at, the better I get.

Q.   By looking at so many charts, obviously you must see lots of stocks take off or implode (for shorts). By missing these setups, doesn't this irritate you?

A.   It used to. Now it just motivates me to see if I could have caught it ahead of time. This makes me a better chart reader.

Q.   You said you set up your quote screen with alarms "near" your entries. Why not at your entries?

A.   When a stock triggers, especially if it's an obvious setup, it can move awfully fast. I want to know when it's getting close to triggering. I don't want to know after the fact.

Q.   Do you ever enter before the trigger?

A.   If the markets are really in gear, then I might attempt to enter early and use a tighter-than-normal stop and look to re-enter if stopped out. Conversely, if the overall environment is mediocre, I might let setups trigger and wait to see if they follow through or possibly wait for a second entry.

Q.   For your own scans, do you have parameters to reduce the number of stocks that fit the pattern?

A.   Yes. My goal with my scans is to show me the best setups on the best stocks. Often, I'll use historical volatility and ADX as filters along with minimum volume requirements.

Q.   Where do you set these parameters?

A.   I normally set the average volume to 100,000 or higher. For the HV, I normally keep it above 40 but may raise it to as high as 80 depending on market conditions. ADX, when used, also varies. I'll usually keep it at 25 or higher, but raise or lower that threshold depending on overall market conditions.

Q. You mentioned you look at the futures market. The indices and bond market makes sense, why other commodities?

A. It all depends on the situation. If crude oil is at 10-year highs and it looks like it's going even higher, then that will likely drive interest rates higher and affect the indices. Markets are interrelated. For instance, in the summer of 2000, someone joked on Bloomberg that if you predict the stock market, the euro and the crude oil market, then you can trade bonds.

Q. Are there any fixed relationships?

A. There used to be. For instance, you could pretty much predict the bond market with the stock market and vice versa. Now, it seems that the relationships only matter when traders decide to fixate on them. However, they're still worth watching.

Q. You mentioned you check to see if the stocks you are interested in are optionable. What are you looking for here?

A. If the options are cheap enough, *occasionally*, I might just buy options versus the underlying stock or, I know that I might be able to use them to hedge, should I be blessed with a profit. I also look to see if there is a large open interest in a particular strike, especially when expiration is near.

Q. Some traders stress the importance of writing down market stats, forcing them to recognize market conditions. Do you do a similar exercise daily?

A. This is a wonderful exercise. One of the most successful traders I know wakes up early each morning and fills out a sheet of about 50 market statistics. He has done this religiously for the past 30 years.

In the past, I used to keep daily stats. In fact, I have tons of notebooks full of market data lying around my office collecting dust. I would recommend anyone getting started to do similar exercises. Due to time constraints, I now lean on my computer to keep the database for me. I will note any anomalies or extremes in my trading journal.

Q. Such as?

A. If the VIX is at an extremely low level historically, I'll make a note of it and take notes on what it has done in the past during similar conditions. Things like this often become an early warning system.

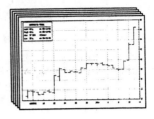

CHAPTER **15**

MORE EXAMPLES

. . . .

MONEY-MANAGEMENT EXAMPLES

On 07/14/2000, Immunex Corp. (IMNX) sets up as a simple four-bar deep pullback.

FIGURE 15.1

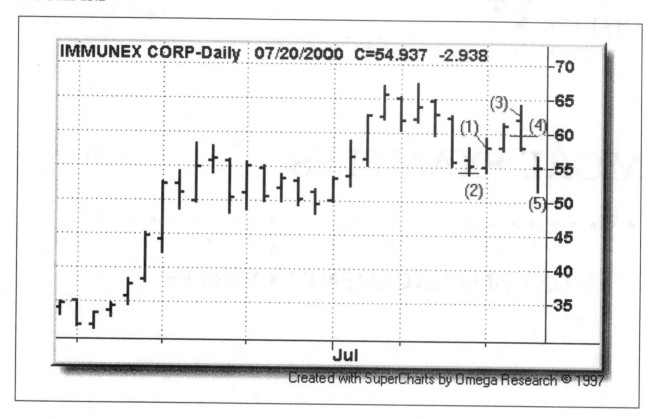

1. An entry on 07/15/2000 is triggered at 57 15/16, 1/16 above the prior day's high.

2. Because the low of the formation is more than 5% away from the entry, a protective stop is placed at 54 15/16 for a 3-point risk (approximately a 5% risk).

3. IMNX rallies over 3 points to 60 15/16 and we exit half of our position.

4. The protective stop is moved up to breakeven (57 15/16, the same as the entry), and we are stopped out for a scratch on the remainder of the position.

5. The market gaps lower and trades below our original entry. As you can see, if money management was not used, this overall profitable trade would have resulted in a loss.

On 07/20/2000, Viratra (VRTA) sets up as a simple three-bar pullback.

FIGURE 15.2

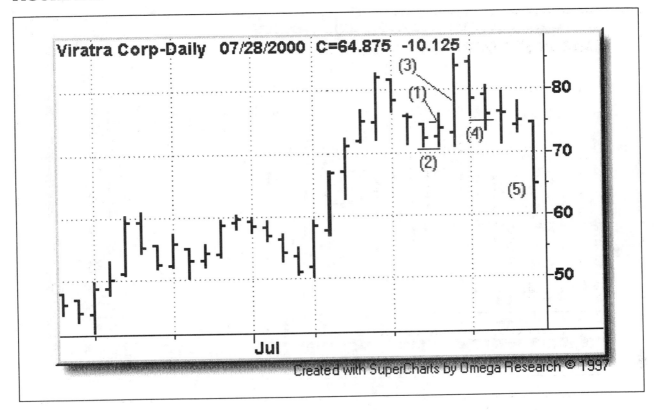

1. An entry at 74 7/16 is triggered, 1/16 above the prior day's high.

2. Set a protective stop at 71 1/16, 1/16 below the low of the setup for a risk of 3 3/8 points.

3. VRTA hits our profit target of 77 15/16. We exit half of our position for a profit of 3 3/8 and move our protective stop on the remaining shares to breakeven (1). Note: On such a wide-range bar, you might want to exit additional shares.

4. The stock trades at 74 7/16 and we are out for a scratch on the remaining shares.

5. The stock implodes. As you can see, what could have been a losing trade is modestly profitable due to money management.

Anadigics (ANAD) sets up as a Double Top Knockout (DT-KO).

FIGURE 15.3

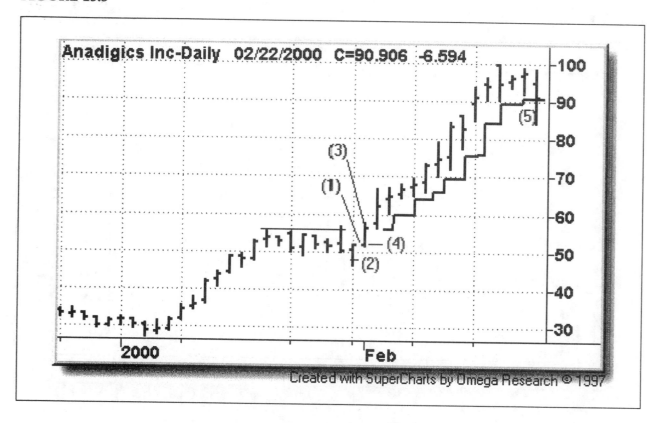

1. The stock triggers an entry at 52 1/16.

2. The low of the setup bar is more than 5% away from our entry, so we place our protective stop at 49 7/16 for a risk of approximately 5% (2 5/8 points).

3. The stock rallies to 54 11/16 and we lock in half of the profits for a 2 5/8-point gain.

4. We move our stop to breakeven (the same as the entry).

5. Trail a stop higher. Here we used a simple two-bar low. As swing traders we would look to continue to scale out of the position as it continues to move in our favor and would likely have been out by the end of the seventh day. For those willing to stay in the market for extended periods, you could have trailed a stop on a piece of the position. In this case, this simple trailing-stop technique would have kept you in for a 38-point run.

TREND QUALIFIERS
AND SETUP EXAMPLES

FIGURE 15.4

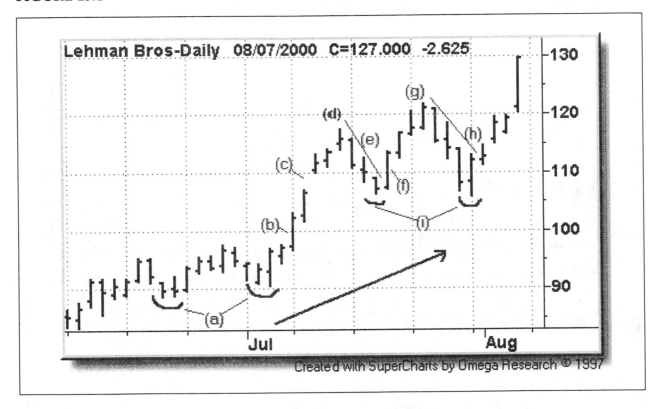

a. Lehman Brothers, a stock in a strong uptrend, forms a High-Level Micro Double Bottom.

b. The stock breaks to new highs on an expansion of range.

c. The stock gaps to new highs—another momentum clue.

d. New highs again.

e. The stock begins to pull back forming a three-bar pullback and a Simple Pullback.

f. The stocks resumes its uptrend on an expansion of range

g. New highs.

h. A four-bar deep pullback (Snapback).

i. High-Level Micro Double Bottom.

FIGURE 15.5

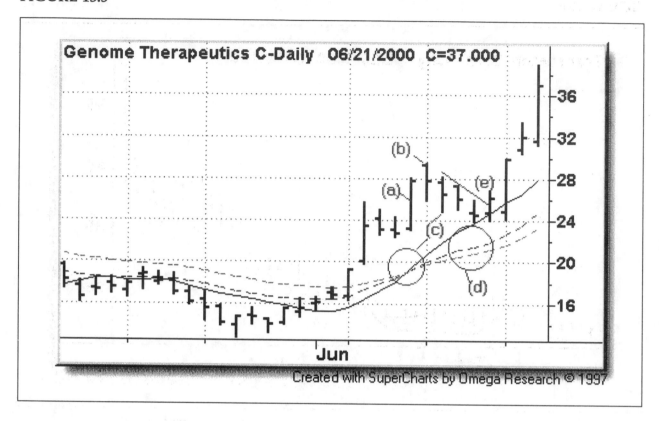

a. Genome Therapeutics (GENE) has a wide-range bar higher and strong close.

b. The stock gaps to a two-month high.

c. A Bow Tie forms: the moving averages converge and then spread out again combined with a lower low.

d. Positive slope in the moving averages.

e. An entry for the Bow Tie, which is also a simple three-bar pullback from highs.

FIGURE 15.6

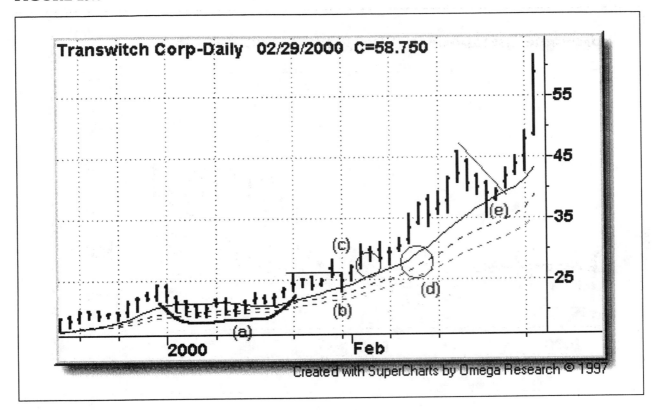

a. Transwitch (TXCC) forms a high-level "running saucer."

b. Double Top Knockout.

c. The trend resumes . . . Daylight.

d. Positive slope in the moving averages.

e. Simple four-bar pullback.

FIGURE 15.7

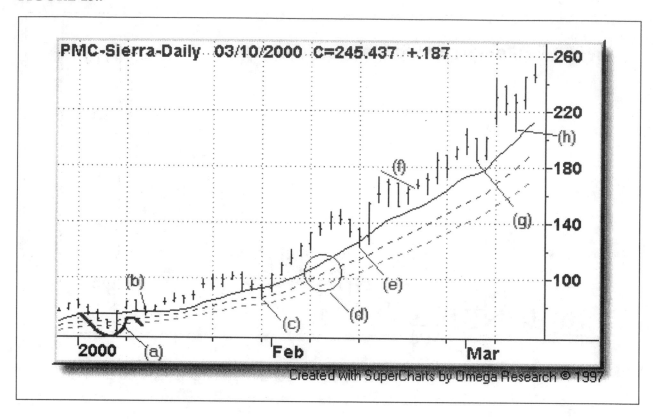

a. PMC-Sierra makes new highs and forms a high-level micro cup and handle.

b. This also sets up as a Double Top Knockout.

c. Trend Knockout.

d. Positive slope on moving averages and Daylight.

e. Trend Knockout

f. Simple three-bar pullback.

g. Trend Knockout

h. Trend Knockout

FIGURE 15.8

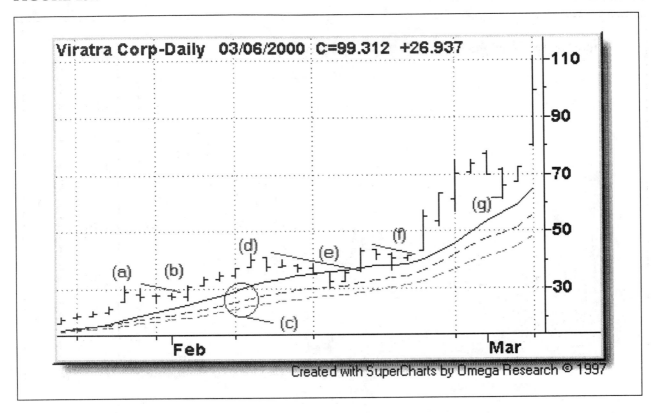

a. Viratra Corp., a stock in a strong uptrend, makes a new high.

b. Three-bar pullback.

c. Positive slope in 10-SMA, 20-EMA and 30-EMA. Also, Daylight (lows greater than moving averages).

d. New High.

e. Simple six-bar pullback.

f. Simple three-bar pullback.

g. Trend Knockout.

FIGURE 15.9

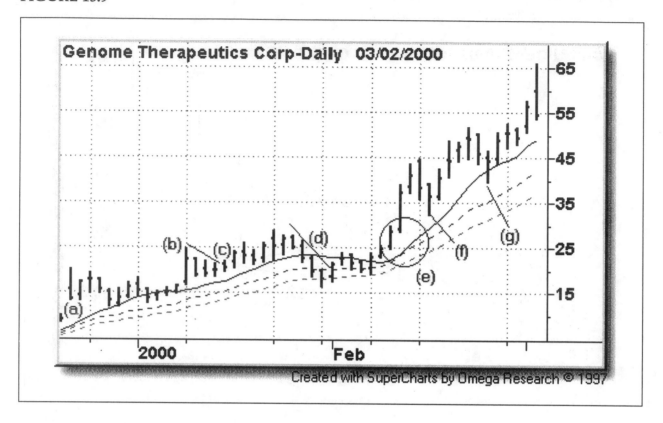

a. Daylight.

b. Wide-range bar higher/base breakout.

c. Three-bar pullback.

d. Another pullback.

e. Daylight, positive slope.

f. Trend Knockout (TKO).

g. TKO.

FIGURE 15.10

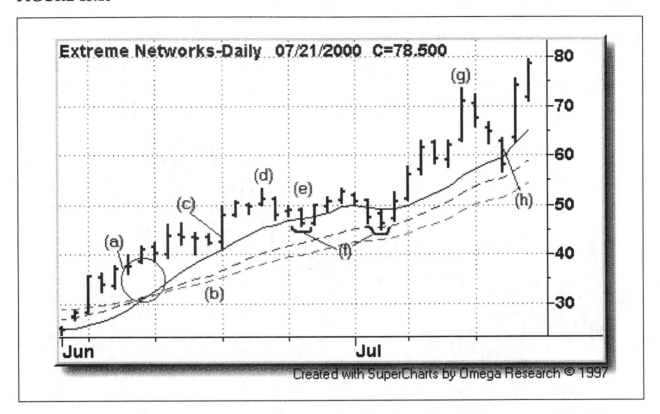

a. Daylight.

b. Positive slope in moving averages and 10-SMA > 20-EMA > 30-EMA (proper order).

c. Bow Tie entry, new two-month high on expansion of range.

d. Another new high.

e. Simple three-bar pullback.

f. High-Level Micro Double Bottom.

g. New two-month high on expansion of range.

h. Deep pullback (Snapback).

Here we have an example in the Technology SPDRs ("Spiders").

FIGURE 15.11

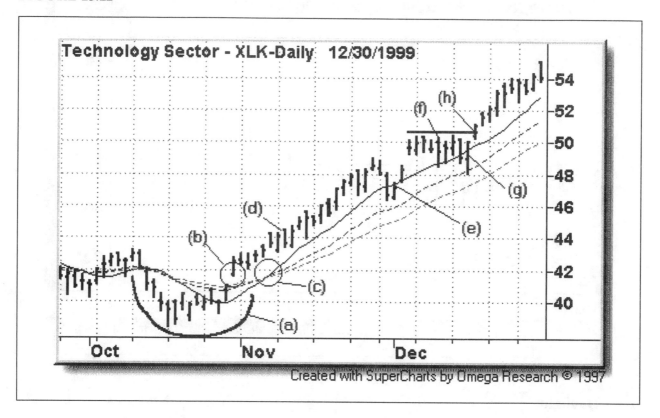

a. The Tech Spiders (XLK) form a cup.

b. Daylight (lows greater than moving averages).

c. Moving averages converge and then spread out forming a Bow Tie. Also, moving averages now in proper uptrend order (10-SMA>20-EMA>30-EMA).

d. Bow Tie entry.

e. Simple three-bar pullback.

f. Trend Knockout (TKO).

g. Another Trend Knockout. Very similar to Double Top Knockout.

h. Base breakout.

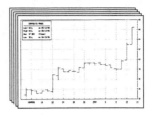

CHAPTER **16**

MORE THOUGHTS

◘ ◘

Q.   Why write this book?

A.   It's funny. Trading is about the only profession in which you get criticized for writing a book. I suppose it's because the business is a competitive one and not a cooperative one. I'll admit that I did write it for the obvious reasons: ego and money. It would be great to be known as an authority on swing trading. Making some money in the process doesn't hurt either. However, there's something over and above the obvious. I have struggled for years to become a successful trader. There were times during extended drawdowns when I felt completely worthless. In spite of all my formal education, during these periods I felt like about all I was good for was flipping burgers. Knowing how painful this is, I would hate to see any struggling trader go through this process. My intent was to write a complete manual that any trader serious about being successful could follow. Also, though it was not my original intent, soon after I began writing, this manual became a manual for me. It forced me to realize when I was violating my own rules. Putting everything down in writing cemented the process. In fact, 90% of my losing trades while writing this book occurred when I didn't follow my own rules.

Q.   Are you worried that someone will come in, take your patterns and eradicate the edge?

A.   My patterns are all designed for swing trades. Large traders and institutions can't make money on this time frame. Due to their size, they have to scale in over a period of days to weeks. Also, if someone has achieved the status of a "large trader" or institution, chances are they have their own ways of doing things. They're not going to run out and read a book and apply the concepts. One last point: most people when they read about a method don't follow it to a "T." They put their own twist on it.

Q.   What would you suggest to a beginner who's dedicated to learning how to trade?

A.   First and foremost, they should learn as much as possible about money management. Memorize the drawdown charts. Know that if you lose half of your money, it'll take a 100% gain to get back to breakeven. Look at charts, lots of charts. Find something simple and stick with it. Also, be optimistic but realistic. Some of the best money managers in the world, on average, only return between 20% and 30% per year, but do so with very minimal drawdowns year in and year out.

Q.   Are there any traits in beginning traders that would suggest to you that they will eventually become successful?

A.   We're all setup junkies, so most that approach me have questions about patterns and charts. However, when someone asks me a money management question, I have the utmost respect for him or her. I immediately think, now here's a guy (or gal) who's going to be successful. Hard work is also vitally important. Trading, on the surface, looks like the complete life of leisure. You click a few keys, rake in the cash and then go sit on your yacht to count your money. In reality, it's a lot of hard work. I have yet to meet a successful trader who puts in fewer hours than those in the corporate world. I was once at a seminar surrounded by six traders who were dying to know how I go about finding stocks to trade. I explained to them that I first tool through about 600 charts after the close. Four of the "traders" looked at each other, shook their heads and walked off. I suppose they expected me to say, "Oh, I run a magic scan and then I'm off to the beach." The two remaining individuals began to berate me with questions: "What charting software do you use?" "Who is your data vendor?" "How fast is your computer?" "How big are your monitors?" and so on and so forth. If I had to put money on who would be successful out of the six, I think I know which two to bet on.

Q. You have many setups. Do you trade them all?

A. Obviously, everything doesn't set up every day. But, yes, unlike many who publish patterns for the sake of publishing, I use every pattern in this manual either directly in trading or in helping me develop a game plan for trading.

Q. What setups do you mostly focus on?

A. I focus mostly on the basics, which is covered in the first section of the manual. In fact, this probably makes up about 90% of what I do. The rest is based on more advanced concepts.

Q. Referring to your advanced techniques. Are there any patterns that you will almost always take?

A. On the more rare patterns, such as the Double Top Knockout, I'll watch for entries. I suppose this is because not too many stocks set up at any given time making it easy to track. Also, I'll strongly consider any pattern that sets up as a combination such as a shallow pullback in a low volatility situation.

Q. Do you trade every day?

A. Because I write a nightly analysis for TradingMarkets.com, I'm forced to do my homework. Through this, I can *usually* find something worthwhile. However, if I encounter a string of losses, I'll back way off and possibly even quit for a while until I can figure out if it's me or the markets.

Q. What percentage of your trades are correct?

A. In trading the results are skewed. It can get really streaky. There are times when I will go weeks on end and 90% to 100% of my trades are winners. Other times, it's just the opposite. You have to realize that the *majority* of your profits come from the *minority* of trades. If I had to come up with an average, I'd say about 50% to 60%. But, I no longer worry about being right, instead I focus on making money.

Q. Your examples show exactly where to get in and exactly where to place your protective stops. Can you elaborate more on what to do *af-*

ter you've entered and placed your stops? In other words, how to manage the position.

A.   The secret to position management is taking half of your profits once they are equal to or greater than your initial risk and then moving your stop to breakeven (2-for-1 Money Management). This will generate income for your account. This income is vital to long-term survival, as it will help to cover the inevitable and often frequent small losses associated with swing trading.

Q.   Okay, suppose you are fortunate enough to have taken half profits and you have moved your stop on your remaining shares to breakeven. How do you manage the remainder of the position?

A.   You're in a great place from both a psychological and financial position once you have moved your stop to breakeven. This is the easy part. I look to do two things: continue to scale out and trail stops. If I'm lucky enough to get a parabolic move (e.g., a sharp move higher in a long position) then by all means, I take most, if not all of it.

Q.   You didn't talk much about trailing stops. Can you elaborate?

A.   It's really not rocket science. One of my favorite techniques is to trail a stop below the lowest low of the prior two bars (for longs). So if on Monday the low is 98 and the low for Tuesday is 100, then going into Wednesday, I'll ratchet my stop up to 97 15/16, right below the lowest of the two prior days. I have an example of this under More Examples (Chapter 15).

Q.   What about time stops?

A.   After five or six days I find my patience starts to wane. I'm usually out by the seventh day unless I'm fortunate enough to be in a strong trend. At this point, I'll continue to trail a stop.

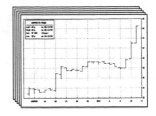

CHAPTER **17**

READY, SET, WAIT!

▫ ▫

This manual is the culmination of over 10 years of research, market analysis and trading. I strongly believe that I have included everything that a swing trader needs in order to take on the markets and be successful. This is not to say that you should run out and try all of the methods and concepts immediately. Ease into it, especially if you are fairly new to trading. Study each pattern and setup in this book. If it makes sense to you, research it and find historical setups. Which ones worked? Which ones didn't? What were the market dynamics at that time? What were the sector dynamics? Is there a modification to the setup that would lend itself more to your style of trading? Are there money-management techniques you could implement that would allow you to control risk or capture larger profits? Once you've done your homework, then paper trade method(s). Be a realist and carefully document your records—timestamp your "trades" or use a tracking service.

After you have completed the above due diligence, make sure you go through one final checklist before jumping into the markets:

What is the setup?

Where is your entry?

Where is your protective stop?

Where will you look to scale out?

What is the overall market doing?

>Are there any systems that are triggering?

>Is there momentum?

>Are there any setups that are triggering?

What is the sector doing?

>Is there momentum?

>Are there any setups that are triggering?

Are you focused, free of distractions and of sound body and mind?

After you have answered all of the above, you should be ready to face the markets.

CHAPTER **18**

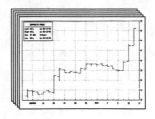

CLOSING THOUGHTS

▪ ▫ ▪ ▫ ▪ ▫ ▪ ▫ ▪ ▫ ▪ ▫ ▪ ▫ ▪ ▫ ▪ ▫ ▪ ▫ ▪ ▫ ▪ ▫ ▪

As I complete this manual in late 2000, many of the biggest and best names associated with a "buy and hold" portfolio have been decimated. Home Depot, Intel, Microsoft and America Online are down over 50% from their highs; Yahoo! and AT&T have lost over 60% of their value since the beginning of the year; Lucent (LU) has lost over 70% of its value during the same period and Apple Computer is 80% off its highs. The list goes on and on.

My method of swing trading allows you to a) participate in the best names at the most opportune times and b) when wrong, avoid being caught in debacles such as those listed above.

Best of luck with your trading!

Dave Landry

P.S. Protective stops on every trade!

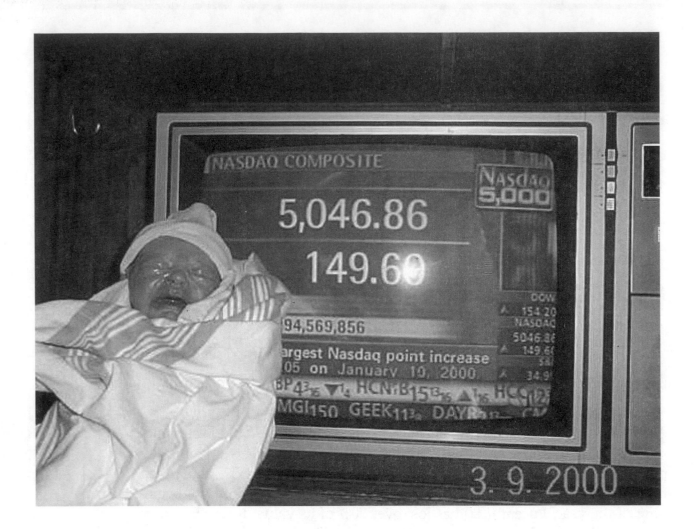

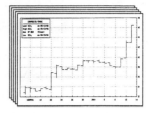

APPENDIX

■ ■

FORMULAS

While the following formula for historical volatility may be of use to a mathematician, you should ideally have a software program calculate this for you.

CALCULATING HISTORICAL VOLATILITY

Let *Length* = length of volatility to be calculated
and *ln* = natural logarithm

Historical Volatility(length) = standard deviation(ln(close/yesterday's close),length) * 100 * square root (256).

In English:

1. Divide today's close by yesterday's close.

2. Take the natural log of #1.

3. Take the standard deviation of #2 for length desired (the number of trading days, i.e. 50)

4. Multiply #3 by 100.

5. Multiply #4 by the square root of the number of trading days in 1 year (around 256).

GLOSSARY

The following terms are used throughout this manual. Even if you are a more advanced trader, you might want to skim this chapter to see how they are defined for purposes of this manual.

Average Directional Movement Index (ADX)—Developed by Welles Wilder, this formula is used to measure the strength of a market but not its direction. The higher the reading, the stronger the trend, regardless if it is up or down. It is calculated based on the Positive Directional Movement Index (+DMI) and Minus Directional Movement Index (-DMI). See +DMI, -DMI, "Capturing Trends Through ADX" in this appendix for more information.

Bar Chart—Shows the open, high, low and close of a market.

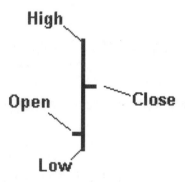

Downtrend—A series of lower lows and lower highs.

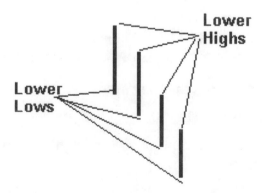

+DMI—see Plus Directional Movement Index.

–DMI—see Minus Directional Movement Index.

Exponential Moving Average—A moving average that gives higher weighting to more recent prices.

Fading—Trading contrary to the trend.

Gap Down—Today's open is less than yesterday's low.

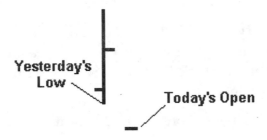

Gap Up—Today's open is greater than yesterday's high.

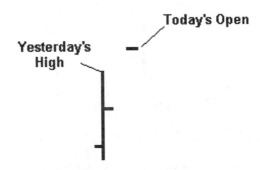

Higher High—Today's high is greater than yesterday's high.

Higher Low—Today's low is greater than yesterday's low.

Historical Volatility—A statistical measurement of how much prices have fluctuated in the past. It can be used to measure risk and potential reward. See Chapter 4, Stock Selection, Section Three, Volatility and the Appendix for more details.

Initial Protective Stop—An order placed right after a trade is entered to help control risk.

Lap Down—Today's open is less than yesterday's close but not less than yesterday's low.

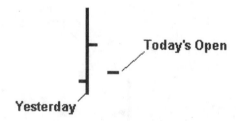

Lap Up—Today's open is greater than yesterday's close but not greater than yesterday's high.

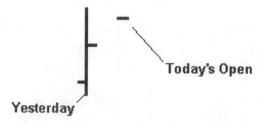

Limit Order—An order to buy or sell at a specified price.

Long—A position that seeks to profit if the market rises. To buy.

Lower High—Today's high is less than yesterday's high.

Lower Low—Today's low is less than yesterday's low.

Market Order—An order to be executed immediately at the asking price for buys and at the bid price for sales.

Minus Directional Movement Index (–DMI)—A component used in the calculation of ADX that measures the downward movement of a market. If it is greater than the Positive Directional Movement, it suggests a downtrend.

Moving Average—The average price of a stock over a given period. For instance, a 10-day moving average would be the sum of those prices divided by 10. See Chapter 3, Trend Qualifiers for more details.

Outside Day—Today's high is *greater than* yesterday's high and today's low is *less than* yesterday's low.

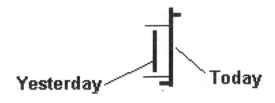

Pivot High—A high surrounded by two *lower* highs. Can also be two equal (or in rare cases three) highs surrounded by two lower highs.

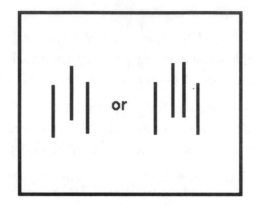

Pivot Low—A low surrounded by two *higher* lows. Can also be two equal (or in rare cases three equal) lows surrounded by two *higher* lows.

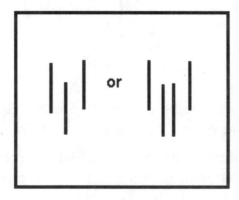

Poor Close—The market closes in the bottom 25% of its range.

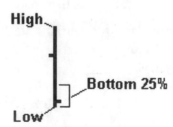

Plus Directional Movement Index (+DMI)—A component used in the calculation of ADX that measures the upward movement of a market. If it is in greater than the Negative Directional Movement Index (–DMI), it suggests an uptrend.

Protective Buy Stop—Used to help control losses when shorting stocks. The order is placed *above* the current price of the stock. It becomes a market order if the stock trades at or above the specified price.

Protective Sell Stop—Used to help control losses when buying stocks. The order is placed *below* the current price of a stock. It becomes a market order if the stock trades at or below the specified price.

Range—The high price of the day minus the low price of the day. See also True Range.

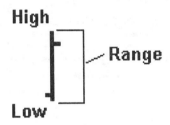

Sell Short—A position that seeks to profit if a market drops in value. See "Selling Short: The Art of Playing Both Sides of The Market" in this Appendix for more details.

Stop Order—For buys, an order placed above the current stock price that becomes a market order if the stock trades at or above the order price. For sells, an order placed below the current price of the stock that becomes a market order if the market trades at or below the order price. Stop orders are normally used to help control risk but can also be used to enter positions.

Strong Close—The stock closes within the top 25% of its range.

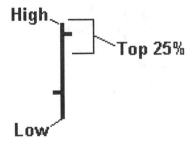

Trailing Stop—A stop adjusted higher for long positions or lower for short positions as the market moves in the favor of the trade. Used to help lock in profits for when the market reverses.

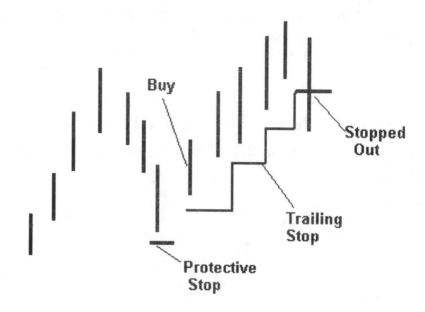

True Range—Conceived by Welles Wilder and used in the ADX calculation, the true range is the same as range except that gaps (if they exist) are used in the calculation.

True range is the largest value (in absolute terms) of:

1. today's high and today's low

2. today's high and yesterday's close

3. today's low and yesterday's close

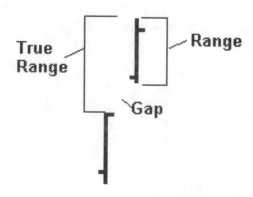

Uptrend—A series of higher highs and higher lows. See Chapter 3, Trend Qualifiers for more details.

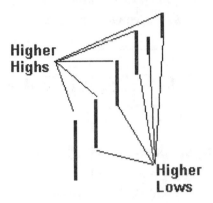

Volatility—How much prices fluctuate over time.

I originally published the following article on shorting stocks on TradingMarkets.com in January 1999. To my surprise, it quickly became one of the most popular articles and has since been re-published by other Internet sites. Special thanks to Larry Connors, CEO of TradingMarkets.com, for allowing me to re-publish this article.

SHORTING STOCKS: THE ART OF PLAYING BOTH SIDES OF THE MARKET

To the public, selling stocks short can be an intimidating and confusing undertaking. Unfortunately, by sticking exclusively to the long side of the market, average traders deny themselves the possibility of improving their returns.

Professional traders, by contrast, know playing both sides of the market is a crucial element of long-term stock trading success. We will try to de-mystify the process by explaining what short selling is and how you can benefit from incorporating it into your trading plan. We'll also show you the rules that regulate short selling, and how to know which stocks to avoid.

REVERSING THE RULES

When many people think of stock trading they automatically imagine buying a stock and hoping it goes up. When it does, they envision selling it and pocketing a profit. For example, suppose XYZ company was trading at $10 per share. You would buy your shares at $10 (a "long" position) and sell them later at $12. Your profit from the trade would be the difference between your entry and exit prices: $12 – $10, a $2-per-share profit. Nothing complicated here.

But what about when a market is falling? Short selling is simply a matter of reversing the process described in the previous paragraph to profit when a stock drops. For instance, suppose XYZ was trading at $12 but you thought the stock would drop and you sold instead of bought—that is, you "shorted" the market. If you later bought your shares back at $10, you would still have a $2-per-share profit.

Your trade consists of the same transactions (a buy and a sell) and nets the same profit. The only difference is that in the case of the short sale, you sell the stock first and buy it back later—hopefully at a lower price than where you originally sold it.

WHY SHORT STOCKS?

The advantage to selling stocks short is simple: Bull markets do not last forever, and even in the longest bull market there are corrections that last from as little as a several minutes to as long as several months. Professional traders seize these downside opportunities and profit by shorting stocks. Therefore, if you want to make a long-term living trading the stock market, it is to your advantage to add short selling to your toolbox.

WHAT IT MEANS TO SELL SHORT

In a short selling situation, you enter a position without owing the stock. How can you sell something you do not own? The answer is, you can't. You have to borrow it before you can sell it. For example, suppose you borrowed what you think is a cheap plate from a neighbor. Now suppose someone was visiting you and offered you $100 for the plate. You recognize that $100 is much more than this plate is worth, so you sell it to him. But now you owe your neighbor his plate—you are, in essence, short one plate. As long as you can replace it for less than $100, you make a profit.

Many people have a problem with selling before buying-it just seems to fly in the face of what is "natural." But the short-selling process is really no different than when you order something and place a deposit. The salesman to whom you paid the deposit is "short" the product he owes you. As long as he can fill your order for less than what you have agreed to pay for it, he makes a profit. From the salesman's perspective, the deposit ensures you will keep up your end of the bargain.

Short selling stocks is a similar process. If you believe a stock is over-valued, you put up a deposit (to cover potential losses) and instruct your broker to sell the shares short. To do this, he borrows the shares from another account and sells them in the market. You are now short the stock. As long as you can buy it back for less than what you sold it, you will make a profit.

RULES AND REGULATIONS

The Securities and Exchange Commission (SEC) has established specific rules regulating the short sale of stocks. First, you must have a margin/short account with your broker. Second, the shares for the stock you wish to short must be available to borrow. Third, you can only sell short on an up tick. Finally, you must have (and maintain) at least 50 percent (or more, see below) of the stock's value in your account.

Let's break it down:

1. *You must have a margin and short account agreement with your broker.*

A "margin" account allows you to use stocks you own as collateral; a "short" account allows you to short stocks. This agreement also allows your broker to "borrow" shares from you should other traders wish to short a stock you own.

2. *The stock must be available to borrow.*

Your broker must be able to borrow the shares from someone else's account. If he cannot, no short sale is allowed. Shorting stocks without first borrowing the shares is known as "naked shorting" and is illegal.

3. *The stock must trade on an up tick.*

This means that the stock must tick higher before they will allow you to short the stock. If you attempt to short a stock that trades at $50, $49 3/4, $49 1/2, and $49 5/8, your short trade would not be executed until the first higher trade in the sequence ($49 5/8). (This rule was instituted to keep short sellers from manipulating the market.) You also can short sell on an "equal tick" if the preceding trade was an up tick. For example, if the stock traded at $50, $49 3/4, $49 1/2, $49 5/8, and again at $49 5/8, you could short sell on the second trade at 49 5/8-you would not have to wait for the stock to up tick again to 49 11/16. Note: as of late 2000, this rule may be repealed.

4. *You must maintain at least 50 percent of the stock's value in your account.*

This deposit is required in order to cover potential losses. Just as a salesman requires a deposit on something you special order, the brokers (and the SEC) require that you maintain at least 50 percent of the stock's value in your account in case your position turns into a loser. If the stock begins to rise you would have to add more money to your account (or exit the position). Conversely, if the stock began to drop you could remove excess cash (or use it for other transactions) as long as you maintained at least the 50 percent margin in your account.

While 50 percent is the absolute minimum deposit that brokerages will accept, some brokers may require a larger deposit. Also, because volatile stocks are riskier, brokerages may require additional margin on these issues for extra insurance.

SHORT-SELLING STRATEGIES

In general, the majority of patterns that work on the long side of the market also work (in reverse) on the short side. For instance, just as from new highs often present good buy opportunities, pullbacks from lows often present opportunities to sell short.

STOCKS TO AVOID

Just because something appears overvalued does not mean it cannot go higher. Many traders were devastated by shorting "overvalued" biotech stocks in the early 1990s and by shorting "overvalued" Internet stocks in the late 1990s. This is not to say you should avoid hot sectors all together; it is just a warning to be cautious and realistic about the possibility of sustained stock rallies.

You should always ask your broker if a particular stock you are interested in is hard to borrow. Avoid such stocks because you could easily get caught in what is known as a "short squeeze," which occurs when a stock rallies and the short sellers are forced to cover (exit) their positions. This demand far exceeds the supply and pushes the stock much higher. If you believe a hard-to-borrow stock is headed lower, you are much better off buying a put option.

SUMMARY

Shorting stocks allows you to enter the market as a seller and profit when a stock declines. Your broker "borrows" the stock from someone else's margin/short account and sells it in the market for you. As long as you buy back the shares at a lower price, you will profit.

To short stocks you must first establish a margin/short account with your broker. The stock you wish to short must be available to borrow and you must maintain at least 50 percent or more of the stock's value in your account. Also, you can sell stock short only on an up tick.

Professional traders sell stocks short because they know markets are prone to corrections and longer-term declines. Many of the techniques that work on the long side of the market also work (in reverse) on the short side. Finally, avoid hard-to-borrow stocks and be cautious about shorting stocks in a hot sector.

CAPTURING TRENDS WITH THE ADX

The Average Directional Movement Index (ADX) measures the trend strength of a market but not its direction. The higher the ADX reading, the stronger the trend, regardless if it is up or down.

The ADX, which was developed by Welles Wilder, uses calculations called the positive directional movement index (+DMI) and minus directional movement index (–DMI) to measure price movement. Although the entire ADX calculation is somewhat lengthy and complex, understanding the basis of the calculation—directional movement—is fairly straightforward and will help you understand how the indicator works.

Below we will show you how to determine the directional movement and interpret ADX readings.

UNDERSTANDING DIRECTIONAL MOVEMENT

Directional movement is essentially the part of a price bar that falls outside of the prior price bar's range. In terms of a daily chart, price action above yesterday's high is positive directional movement (+DM), while anything below yesterday's low is negative directional movement (–DM).

FIGURE A.1

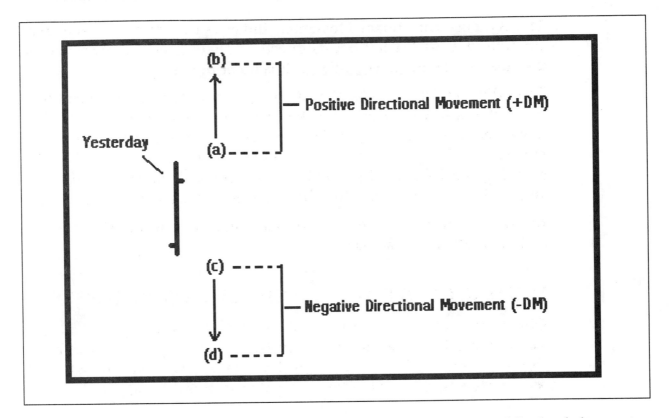

Directional Movement (DM). Price action above yesterday's high is +DM while that below yesterday's low is –DM.

In Figure A.1, notice the box *a-b* above yesterday's price. For today, anything above yesterday's high (for instance, if the market trades from *a* to *b* is +DM. Conversely, anything trading below yesterday's low (for instance, if the market trades from *c* to *d* is –DM.

FIGURE A.2

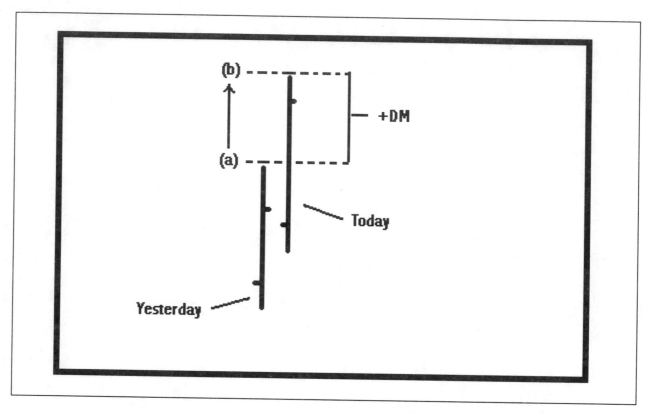

Plus Directional Movement (+DM).

Notice in Figure A.2 that the price bar trades above the prior price bar (from *a* to *b*). This distance is the +DM. Referring to Figure A.3, the range of the bar that trades below the prior day's low (from *c* to *d*) is the –DM.

FIGURE A.3

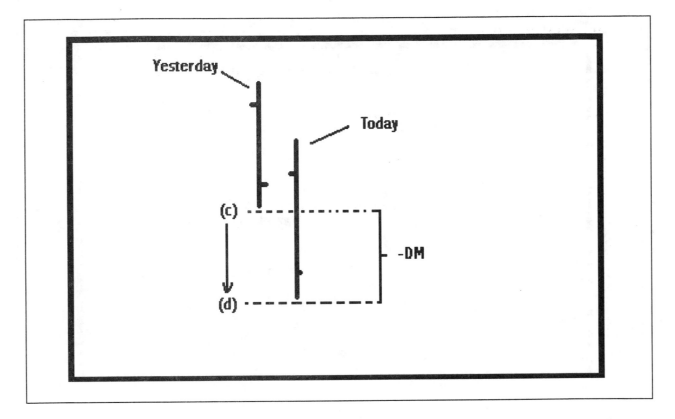

Minus Directional Movement (–DM).

Obviously, not every trading day sets up like Figures A.2 or A.3. Therefore, we must consider two other possibilities: inside days and outside days. An inside day occurs when the entire day's range is "contained" within the prior day's high and low. In other words, today's high is less than yesterday's high and today's low is greater than yesterdays low. For example, if XYZ traded yesterday between 50 and 60 and trades today between 51 and 59, then today is an inside day. In Figure A.4, notice there is no DM (either + or –) because the range doesn't trade above (for a +DM reading) or below (for a –DM reading).

FIGURE A.4

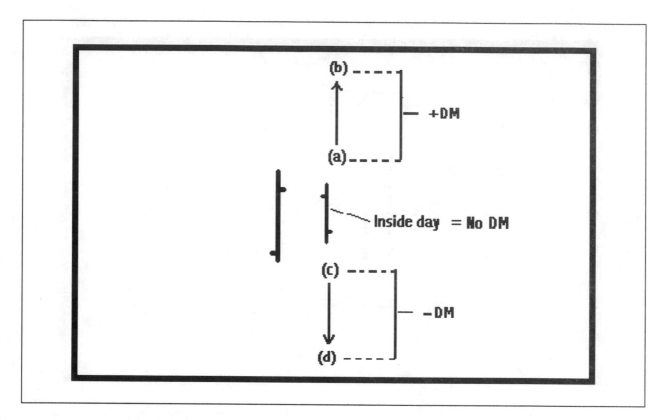

Inside days have no Directional Movement value.

An outside day occurs when today's high is higher than yesterday's high and today's low is lower than yesterday's low. For instance, if XYZ traded between 50 and 55 yesterday and between 49 and 56 today, today is an outside day because today's range is "outside" yesterday's. Because there can only be one directional movement (either + or -) per trading day, the outside day presents an interesting problem because it contains both +DM (today's high greater than yesterday's high) and –DM (today's low less than yesterday's low). Because we are looking to quantify movement in price, on an outside day the largest move—either the difference between today's high and yesterday's high or the difference between yesterday's low and today's low—is the directional movement. This is illustrated in Figure 5. In the rare case that the move above yesterday's high is equal to the move below yesterday's low then there would be no DM for that day.

FIGURE A.5

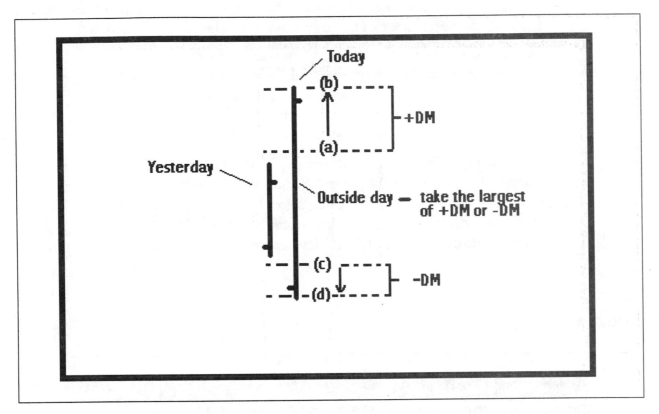

For outside days, the Directional Movement is the greater of the +DM or the –DM.

DIRECTIONAL MOVEMENT (DM) SUMMARY:

1. Today's high > yesterday's high (and today's low > yesterday's low) = +DM

2. Today's low < yesterday's low (and today's high < yesterday's high) = –DM

3. Inside day (today's low > yesterday's low and today's high < yesterday's high) = no DM (either +DM or - DM)

4. For outside days, take the larger of today's high - yesterday's high or yesterday's low - today's low. If these figures are equal, there is no DM.

To make the directional movement readings meaningful for all markets, Wilder divided the DM by the market's *true range*. This creates a directional movement indicator (DMI) in a form of a ratio and allows for meaningful comparisons regardless of various market prices. In other words, the DMI of a $5 stock can be compared to the DMI of a $100 stock.

Because one day does not a trend make, the DMI is then averaged over a number of days. The magnitude of the trend reflected by the ADX—longer-term or shorter-term—depends on the number of days in this calculation. Wilder's default, and the number widely used by charting software packages (and TradingMarkets.com), is 14 days.

The Average Directional Movement Index (ADX) is then calculated by taking the difference between the smoothed +DMI and –DMI calculations. It's obvious the ADX calculation is very complex, but if you understand the directional movement detailed previously, you'll have a good understanding of how the indicator works and enough background to use it.

FIGURE A.6

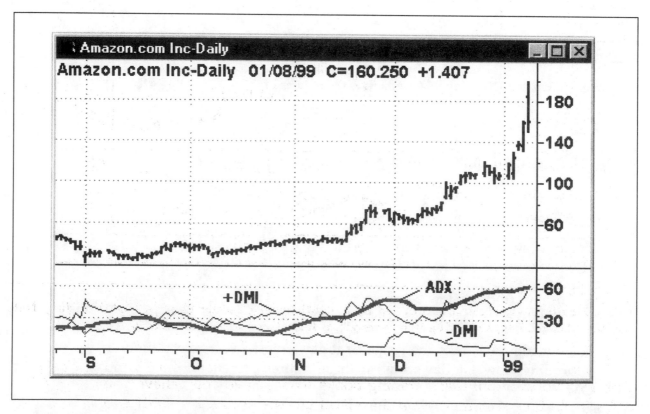

Amazon.com, daily. +DMI greater than –DMI reflects an uptrending market. *Source: Omega Research.*

The ADX measures trend strength but not direction. The direction of the market is determined by comparing the +DMI to the –DMI. If the +DMI is greater than the –DMI the market is in an uptrend; if the –DMI is greater than the +DMI the market is in a downtrend. Referring to Figure A.6, notice that the +DMI is greater than the –DMI signifying and uptrend. Also, notice that the ADX rose to relatively high levels (above 30) as the trend remained strong and the stock quadrupled in value. On the downside, in Figure A.7, notice that the –DMI is greater than the +DMI as the ADX remained above relatively high levels (above 30) as the stock continued to decline.

FIGURE A.7

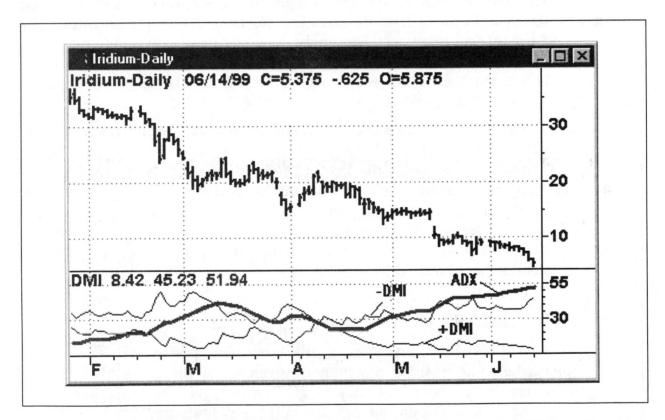

Iridium, daily. A downtrend is reflected by a –DMI reading greater than the +DMI reading. Note that the ADX reading, signifying trend strength, is high. *Source: Omega Research.*

One word of caution: Many trading books would have you believe you can simply buy a market when the +DMI crosses above the –DMI and sell the market when the –DMI crosses below the +DMI. They go on to show well-chosen examples where you could have followed this simple system and made large sums of money. However, nothing could be further from the truth. What they fail to show you is how much money you would lose as the DMIs cross back and forth.

USING THE ADX

High ADX readings reflect a strongly trending market. Conversely, low ADX numbers reflect non-trending markets. The minimum reading to determine a "trend" is subject to debate. In general, 14-day ADX readings above 30 suggest a strongly trending market. Those who only wish to trade the strongest of markets may look for readings of 35 or higher. The trade-off here is that the stronger the number, the longer the trend has been in place. Therefore, much of the original move (that caused the ADX to rise) is missed. Those who look to catch early trends may look for markets with an ADX of 25 or higher. Not surprisingly, the trade-off here is that these markets are more prone to failure because they have yet to "prove" themselves.

The advantage of the ADX is that it provides a standardized way of measuring trend. This lends itself well to computerized scans for finding trending markets (i.e., the TradingMarkets.com ADX Search and Filter). These markets can then be watched for potential entries signals from breakouts, pullbacks, cup-and-handle patterns, and so forth. Counter-trend traders, those who tend to fade markets (trade opposite to the trend) may look to trade markets that are in a trading range or no trending as measured by a low ADX reading.

SUMMARY

The ADX is based on the directional movement, positive or negative of a market. The positive directional movement is the portion of today's range that is above yesterday's high. The negative directional movement is the portion of today's range that falls below yesterday's low.

Only one directional movement is calculated for each day. Therefore, if there are both +DMI and −DMI for a given day (i.e., an outside day) then the larger of the two becomes the directional movement. If today's range does not trade above or below the prior day (i.e., an inside day) then there is no directional movement for that day.

The ADX is calculated by taking the difference of the average directional movement values over a given time period. The ADX measures trend but not direction. The direction of the market is determined by comparing the +DMI to the −DMI. If the +DMI is greater than the −DMI the market is uptrending; if the −DMI is greater than the +DMI the market is downtrending. High ADX readings suggest a market is in a strong trend.

DAVE LANDRY ON SWING TRADING SOFTWARE ADD-ON MODULE: FOR OMEGA TRADESTATION AND SUPERCHARTS 4.0 AND 2000i

STUART OKOROFSKY

This software add-on module for TradeStation and SuperCharts users takes advantage of the ChartScanner (Version 4.0) or Workspace Assistant (Version 2000i) to scan your database of stocks for setups based on the trading strategies from the *Dave Landry on Swing Trading* book. A report is produced listing the name of the stock or commodity, the symbol, the name of the strategy detecting the setup, the recommended entry price and the recommended initial protective stop price.

1 - 3.5" DISKETTE AND INSTRUCTIONS $175.00

HIT AND RUN TRADING

The Short-Term Stock Traders' Bible

JEFF COOPER

Written by professional equities trader, Jeff Cooper, this best-selling manual teaches traders how to day-trade and short-term trade stocks. Jeff's strategies identify daily the ideal stocks to trade and point out the exact entry and protective exit points. Most trades risk 1 point or less and last from a few hours to a few days.

Among the strategies taught are:

- Stepping In Front Of Size—You will be taught how to identify when a large institution is desperately attempting to buy or sell a large block of stock. You will then be taught how to step in front of this institution before the stock explodes or implodes. This strategy many times leads to gains from 1/4 point to 4 points within minutes.

- 1-2-3-4s—Rapidly moving stocks tend to pause for a few days before they explode again. You will be taught the three-day setup that consistently triggers solid gains within days.

- Expansion Breakouts—Most breakouts are false! You will learn the one breakout pattern that consistently leads to further gains. This pattern alone is worth the price of the manual.

- Also, you will learn how to trade market explosions (Boomers), how to trade secondary offerings, how to trade Slingshots, and you will learn a number of other profitable strategies that will make you a stronger trader.

160 PAGES HARD COVER $100.00

STREET SMARTS

High Probability Short-Term Trading Strategies

LAURENCE A. CONNORS AND LINDA BRADFORD RASCHKE

Published in 1996 and written by Larry Connors and *New Market Wizard* Linda Raschke, this 245-page manual is considered by many to be one of the best books written on trading futures. Twenty-five years of combined trading experience is divulged as you will learn 20 of their best strategies. Among the methods you will be taught are:

- **Swing Trading**—The backbone of Linda's success. Not only will you learn exactly how to swing trade, you will also learn specific advanced techniques never before made public.

- **News**—Among the strategies revealed is an intraday news strategy they use to exploit the herd when the 8:30 A.M. economic reports are released. This strategy will be especially appreciated by bond traders and currency traders.

- **Pattern Recognition**—You will learn some of the best short-term setup patterns available. Larry and Linda will also teach you how they combine these patterns with other strategies to identify explosive moves.

- **ADX**—In our opinion, ADX is one of the most powerful and misunderstood indicators available to traders. Now, for the first time, they reveal a handful of short-term trading strategies they use in conjunction with this terrific indicator.

- **Volatility**—You will learn how to identify markets that are about to explode and how to trade these exciting situations.

- Also, included are chapters on trading the smart money index, trading Crabel, trading gap reversals, a special chapter on professional money management, and many other trading strategies!

245 PAGES HARD COVER $175.00

HIT AND RUN TRADING II

CAPTURING EXPLOSIVE SHORT-TERM MOVES IN STOCKS

JEFF COOPER

212 fact-filled pages of new trading strategies from Jeff Cooper. You will learn the best momentum continuation and reversal strategies to trade. You will also be taught the best day-trading strategies that have allowed Jeff to make his living trading for the past decade.

Also included is a special five-chapter bonus section entitled, "Techniques of a Professional Trader," where Jeff teaches you the most important aspects of trading, including money management, stop placement, daily preparation, and profit-taking strategies.

If you aspire to become a full-time professional trader, this is the book for you.

212 PAGES HARD COVER $100.00

THE 5-DAY MOMENTUM METHOD

JEFF COOPER

Strongly trending stocks always pause before they resume their move. *The 5-Day Momentum Method* identifies three- to seven-day explosive moves on strongly trending momentum stocks. Highly recommended for traders who are looking for larger-than-normal short-term gains and who do not want to sit in front of the screen during the day. *The 5-Day Momentum Method* works as well shorting declining stocks as it does buying rising stocks. Also, there is a special section written for option traders.

SPIRAL BOUND $50.00

CONNORS ON ADVANCED TRADING STRATEGIES

31 Chapters on Beating the Markets

LAURENCE A. CONNORS

Written by Larry Connors, this book is broken into seven sections; S&P and stock market timing, volatility, new patterns, equities, day-trading, options, and more advanced trading strategies and concepts. Thirty-one chapters of in-depth knowledge to bring you up to the same level of trading as the professionals.

Among the strategies you will learn are:

- **Connors VIX Reversals I, II and III (Chapter 2)**—Three of the most powerful strategies ever revealed. You will learn how the CBOE OEX Volatility Index (VIX) pinpoints short-term highs and lows in the S&Ps and the stock market. The average profit/trade for this method is among the highest Larry has ever released.

- **The 15 Minute ADX Breakout Method (Chapter 20)**—Especially for day-traders! This dynamic method teaches you how to specifically trade the most explosive futures and stocks every day! This strategy alone is worth the price of the book.

- **Options (Section 5)**—Four chapters and numerous in-depth strategies for trading options. You will learn the strategies used by the best Market Makers and a small handful of professionals to consistently capture options gains!

- **Crash, Burn, and Profit (Chapter 11)**—Huge profits occur when stocks implode. During a recent 12-month period, the Crash, Burn and Profit strategy shorted Centennial Technologies at 49 1/8; six weeks later it was at 2 1/2! It shorted Diana Corp. at 67 3/8; a few months later it collapsed to 4 3/8! It recently shorted Fine Host at 35; eight weeks later the stock was halted from trading at 10! This strategy will be an even bigger bonanza for you in a bear market.

- **Advanced Volatility Strategies (Section 2)**—Numerous, never-before-revealed strategies and concepts using volatility to identify markets immediately before they explode.

- and much, much more!

259 PAGES HARD COVER $150.00

METHOD IN DEALING IN STOCKS

Reading the Mind of the Market on a Daily Basis

JOSEPH H. KERR, JR.

This gem, originally published in 1931 by Joseph Kerr, has been expanded and updated to reflect today's markets. This book is considered to be the bible of interpreting both daily market action and daily news events.

150 PAGES PAPERBACK $35.00

THERE'S ONLY ONE PLACE IN THE WORLD WHERE YOU CAN FIND TRADING INFORMATION LIKE THIS EVERY DAY!

"After one day's trial, I simply subscribed for one year. My $120 dollars was recovered in about one minute."

Girish Patel, M.D.

". . . The idea, concept, roster, presentation, and all the rest are, I believe, absolute winners. Just extraordinary! . . . you destroy, absolutely destroy, TheStreet.com, MarketWatch, Individual Investor, Clearstation, and a host of lesser sites who have instantly become wannabes . . ."

Joel Reingold,
Former Washington correspondent,
TIME magazine

"One of the best (if not the best) traders' websites to date! Thank you!"

Tony Ostrowe

- **In-depth Trading Courses taught by top professional traders**
- **Daily Access to Proprietary Indicators and Strategies**
- **Continuous Intra-day market updates, and instant Market Price Analysis**

- **Interactive Relative Strength searches on over 5,000 stocks**
- **Daily Commentary and Analysis from Professional Traders and Top Hedge Fund Managers**
- **And Much, Much, More!**

SIGN UP NOW FOR YOUR
FREE THREE DAY TRIAL
GO TO WWW.TRADINGMARKETS.COM

ABOUT THE AUTHOR

Dave Landry is a cofounder of and regular contributor to TradingMarkets.com. He is a registered Commodity Trading Advisor (CTA) d/b/a Sentive Trading. He is also a principal of Harvest Capital Management, a hedge fund. Mr. Landry has authored a number of trading systems, including the 2/20 EMA Breakout System and the Volatility Explosion Method, and his articles have been published in *Technical Analysis of Stocks and Commodities, Active Trader and Bridge Trader magazines. His research has been referenced in several books such as Connors On Advanced Trading Strategies* and *Beginners Guide to Computerized Trading.* Mr. Landry holds a Bachelor of Science degree in computer science from the University of Louisiana and a Masters in Business Administration degree from the University of Southern Mississippi.